Keto Air Fryer Recipes

Top 177 Quick, Tasty and Delicious Air Fryer Keto Recipes for Fast and Healthy Meals

Easy Low Carb Air Fryer Recipes to Lose Weight

Michèle COHEN

© 2019 Michèle COHEN

Disclaimer and Terms of Use

Effort has been made to ensure that the information in this book is accurate and complete, however, the author and the publisher do not warrant the accuracy of the information, text and graphics contained within the book due to the rapidly changing nature of science, research, known and unknown facts and internet. The author and the publisher does not hold any responsibility for errors, omissions or contrary interpretation of the subject matter herein. This book is presented solely for motivational and informational purposes only.

Contents

Introduction

Millions of people around the world have discovered that the ketogenic lifestyle is the most effective key to weight loss, disease prevention and intervention, and a more vibrant life. Gone are the days when counting calories was the way to improve one's health, get a slimmer waistline, get rid of disease and look good physically.

The ketogenic diet is not just a great tool to help people lose weight and feel better; it is also an extremely effective method of treating common diseases of civilization. Healthy eating with a ketogenic lifestyle means choosing foods that are nutritionally optimal and providing you with enough carbohydrates to stay healthy, but not enough to weigh you down and sabotage your weight loss or other goals.

By starting to follow the ketogenic lifestyle, you will also learn how to eat to balance your hormones, sleep, feel better and lose weight sustainably.

If you have an air fryer, you already know that it is a revolutionary device designed to save you time and make your life easier. If you still do not make the jump, you'll be excited about how quickly you'll be hooked and using your air fryer to prepare your favorite meals. But what is special about frying in the air?

The air fryer can replace your oven, microwave, deep fryer and dehydrator and allows you to prepare delicious meals in a fraction of the time. If you want to give your family healthy meals, but you do not have much time, the air fryer is a vital part of your kitchen.

An air fryer can make it easy for you to succeed on your ketogenic diet. One of the many benefits of air frying is the short cooking time it provides. This is especially beneficial when you are hungry and want time. The long-term success of a ketogenic diet is often attributed to the ease of preparing healthy and adapted meals. That's why your air fryer will be your best friend throughout your keto trip and help keep you on track, even on days when you're running out of time.

Throughout this book, you will learn all you need to know about how and why to use an air fryer as well as some basics that will help you succeed after a ketogenic diet.

In this book, you will also find recipes designed to obtain perfect ketogenic ratios of lipids, proteins and carbohydrates, in order to train you in ketosis while keeping your body satisfied.

For beginners as well as for ketogenic diet, the 177 recipes and variations of this book is created specifically to please your palate while not forcing you to spend your time in the kitchen! Concise and relevant, the recipes break down the requirements for meal preparation into a simple, step-by-step format, easy to understand by everyone.

This book is well placed to provide you with practical cooking ideas to spice up your daily meals with the air fryer in minutes.

Part 1: Cooking with an Air Fryer

Although this first part of the book covers the basics of using your air fryer, the first step is to read the manual supplied with your air fryer. All air fryers are different and, with the increasing popularity of this device, many models are marketed on the market. Learning how to use your specific air fryer in depth is the key to success and will familiarize you with troubleshooting issues as well as security features. By reading the manual and washing all the parts with hot, soapy water before the first use, you will feel ready to release your culinary finesse!

What is an air fryer?

It is a very simple mechanism of heat circulation that is at the heart of this device. In an air fryer, there is a thermal coil above the removable food container. The container has small holes in its bottom. There is a fan on the thermal coil. The hollow interior wall of the device body is designed so that when the coil is heated and the fan is running, hot air circulates in the food. Thus, the food is well cooked. To maintain the air pressure, there is a small passage on the top of the unit that is controlled by valves. The body of this device is thermally insulated. Thus, the heat transmitted by the coil is used to the maximum to cook your delights. Although this is a new kitchen concept, it is a very effective concept. The function is also very simple but the result is impressive. Its simple mechanism makes it energy efficient. In a deep fryer where the surrounding oil cook food, warm ambient air does the work. So, the food is healthy and tasty at the same time. In addition, the food is very fresh to eat for the process of air circulation.

How to Use Your Air Fryer

Using an air fryer is the most convenient and easy thing to do. Simply take the food container out, place the food, attach the container as it was before and set the timer. The main benefit here is that whichever dish you are preparing you will be needed smallest amount of cooking oil. It is widely advertised and tested that most of the frying in Air Fryer needs as little as a spoon of oil. You can just do require seasoning to your dish and spray little oil on it evenly, take it in the fryer and give required time.

You can find required time in every dish that I included in my book. As it is easy to carry, you can take it anywhere you like. You can even use it in your recreational vehicle to serve your hot delights. You can use it anywhere as long as you can find a useable power source. Taking care of this device is not even can be considered as a matter. The food container is easy to wash and rest of the device doesn't even need any taking care.

This device has a wide range of usability. It can make your French fries crispy outside and perfectly moist inside. It can even cook your steak and fish. You will find me talking about different recipes using it in this book all the time. One thing I can assure you that if you are thinking to invest on an air fryer and a good air fryer recipe book, it will give you the most outcome out of your bucks.

The Benefits of Air Fryer

Air Fryer is all in one in the sense of benefits. It can cook in the least amount of time needed. The foods which are served by making in this device are very well cooked and delicious without being oily. Health-conscious people find it very hard to maintain the oil in food. You can use many time-consuming process to control your oil intake but the best you will find in an air fryer. So instead of frying things in oil, you can have the same crispy taste without spending on oil and your health. The other benefit is that it takes much less time to cook the meal. Approximately half of the time an oven takes. So it is very effective in this manner. It is also efficient in manner of heat use. It is designed in a way that most of the heat produced by the coil is used to cook the food. Heat goes through the food and cooks it evenly. One more benefit in effectiveness is that when it passes some air out to maintain air pressure, it actually filters the air. So you don't have to be suffocated while you cook. It guarantees a good environment outside. It is actually effective in every manner as we think.

You can easily clean this device. The main part to clean here is the food container. You can remove it and wash it as a normal pan. As the rest of the devise does not come in touch with the food so there is no need to clean the other parts. Its portability makes it beyond a home appliance. You can take it with you to anywhere. You just need power and 5 minutes to make your food ready. It is a life saver in this case. So, if the next time it's late at night and you are craving for some spicy food, you can have it before you know that you have cooked.

Why Fry in the Air?

Air frying is becoming more and more popular as it allows you to quickly and evenly prepare delicious meals with little effort. Here are some of the reasons why you want to go for frying in the air:

It replaces other cooking appliances. You can use your air fryer instead of your oven, microwave, deep fryer and dehydrator! In a small device, you can quickly prepare perfect dishes for every meal without sacrificing flavor.

It cooks faster than traditional cooking methods. Air frying works by circulating hot air around the cooking chamber. This results in fast, even cooking using a fraction of the energy in your oven. Most air fryers can be set to a maximum temperature of 400 ° F. For this reason, just about anything you can do in an oven, you can do it in an air fryer.

It uses little or no cooking oil. A main selling point of air fryers is that you can achieve beautifully cooked foods with little to no cooking oil. While that may be attractive to some because it can mean lower fat content, people following the keto diet can rejoice because it means fewer calories, which still matter if you're doing keto for weight loss.

He has a quick cleaning. Regardless of the cooking method used, your stove is dirty, but with the small cooking chamber and the removable basket of your air fryer, deep cleaning is a breeze!

The Functions of an Air Fryer

Most fryers have buttons that allow you to prepare everything, such as to grill the perfect salmon, roast an entire chicken, or even bake a chocolate cake.

These buttons are associated with preset temperatures and times based on your specific air fryer. Due to the wide variety of air fryers on the market, all recipes in this book were created using manual temperatures and temperatures. Each air fryer allows you to adjust yourself. Nevertheless, it is important to know how cooking programs work on your air fryer and when to use them.

Although some recipes for fryers require preheating of the appliance, this is really a personal preference. Some people preheat their air fryer while others add a few minutes to the cooking time, as shown in these recipes. In my experience, preheating has no benefit, so it is not called in this book.

Essential Accessories

The cooking chamber of your fryer is actually just a large open space allowing hot air to circulate. This is a huge advantage because it gives you the opportunity to integrate several different accessories into your kitchen. These accessories increase the number of recipes you can make in your air fryer and offer options you never imagined possible. Here are some of the common accessories.

Metal support. This circular rack is used to add a second layer to your cooking surface so you can maximize space and cook several things at once. This is especially useful when cooking meat and vegetables and you do not want to wait for one to finish to start with the other.

Brochette rack. It looks like a metal stand, but it has metal skewers that make cooking skewers easier.

Ramekin. Small ramekins are perfect for making mini-cakes and quiches. If they go to the oven, they are safe for your air fryer.

Cake mold. You can find cake molds specially designed for your air fryer that fit perfectly into the cooking chamber. They also come with an integrated handle so you can easily remove them when your cakes are cooked.

Pan Cupcake. A cupcake pan usually comes with seven mini-cups and occupies the entire room of your 5.3-quart air fryer. These versatile cups are perfect for muffins, cupcakes and even egg cups. If you do not want to take this route, you can also use individual silicone molds.

Parchment. Especially pre-cut parchments can be useful for easy cleaning when cooking with your air fryer. In addition, you can find parchment paper with pre-cut holes for easy steaming.

Pizza pan. Yes, you can prepare a pizza in your deep fryer and this book contains several recipes for different types of pizzas adapted to keto. It's a great option to easily get the perfect shape every time.

Cleaning Your Fryer

Before cleaning, first make sure your air fryer is completely cold and unplugged. To clean the pan of the fryer, you must:

1. Remove the fryer from the base. Seal the pan with hot water and dishwashing liquid. Let the pan soak in the inside fry basket for 10 minutes.

2. Next, clean the basket thoroughly with a sponge or brush.

3. Remove the basket from the fryer and rub the underside and outer walls.

4. Clean the frying dish with a sponge or brush.

5. Allow to air dry and return to the base of the air fryer.

To clean the outside of your air fryer, simply wipe the outside with a damp cloth. Then make sure all the components are in the right position before starting your next culinary adventure.

Part 2: Keto Air Fryer Recipes

BREAKFAST

Quick and delicious low-carb breakfasts will soon be the norm in your household once you put your air fryer to work! These recipes will kick-start your day in a healthy way without depriving you of the savory goodness mornings should be made of! When you're struggling to get out the door in time, it can be really tough to prepare a nourishing meal for yourself or your family.

The recipes in this chapter are filling and keto-approved, helping you to change your mornings and your entire days. Get ready for nutritious breakfasts that can be made in a flash. With meals you can prepare ahead of time, like Sausage and Cheese Balls, and dishes you can pop in your air fryer to get ready while you get ready, like Quick and Easy Bacon Strips, you'll wish you had started air frying your breakfasts sooner!

Sausage and Cheese Balls

Hands-On Time: **10 minutes**; *Cook Time:* **10 minutes**; *Yield*: **16 balls**.

Ingredients

- 1 pound pork breakfast sausage

- ½ cup shredded Cheddar cheese

- 1 ounce full-fat cream cheese, softened

- 1 large egg

Preparation

1- Mix all ingredients in a large bowl. Train 16 balls (1 inch). Place the balls in the basket of the air fryer.

2- Set the temperature to 400 ° F and set the timer to 12 minutes.

3- Shake the basket two or three times while cooking. Sausage meatballs will be browned on the outside and have an internal temperature of at least 145 ° F when fully cooked.

4- Serve hot.

Nutrition facts per serving

Calories: 424

Fat: 32 g

Protein: 23 g

Carb: 1.6 g

Fiber: 0 g

Spaghetti Squash Fritters

Hands-On Time: **15 minutes**; *Cook Time:* **8 minutes**; *Yield*: **4 servings.**

Ingredients

• 2 cups cooked spaghetti squash

• 2 tablespoons unsalted butter, softened

• 1 large egg

• ¼ cup blanched ground almond flour

• 2 green onion stalks, sliced

• ½ teaspoon of garlic powder

• 1 teaspoon dried parsley

Preparation

1- Remove excess moisture from the squash using a cheesecloth or tea towel.

2- Mix all ingredients in a large bowl. Form into four patties.

3- Cut out a piece of parchment suitable for your air fryer basket. Place each pancake on the parchment and place it in the basket of the air fryer.

4- Set the temperature to 400 ° F and set the timer to 8 minutes.

5- Turn the patties halfway through cooking.

6- Serve hot.

Nutrition facts per serving

Calories: 131

Fat: 10.1 g

Protein: 3.8 g

Carb: 5.1 g

Fiber: 2 g

Buffalo Egg Cups

Hands-On Time: **10 minutes**; *Cook Time:* **15 minutes**; *Yield*: **2 servings.**

Ingredients

• 4 large eggs

• 2 oz. whole cream cheese

• 2 tablespoons buffalo sauce

• ½ cup grated cheddar cheese

Preparation

1- Break eggs in two (4 inches) ramekins.

2- In a small microwave-safe bowl, combine cream cheese, buffalo sauce and cheddar cheese. Microwave for 20 seconds, and then stir. Place a spoonful in each ramekin over the eggs.

3- Place the ramekins in the fryer basket.

4- Set the temperature to 320 ° F and set the timer to 15 minutes.

5- Serve hot.

Nutrition facts per serving

Calories: 354

Fat: 22.3 g

Protein: 21 g

Carb: 2.3 g

Fiber: 0 g

Stuffed Poblano

Hands-On Time: **15 minutes**; *Cook Time:* **15 minutes**; *Yield:* **4 servings.**

Ingredients

- ½ pound spicy ground pork breakfast sausage

- 4 large eggs

- 4 ounces full-fat cream cheese, softened

- ¼ cup canned diced tomatoes and green chiles, drained

- 4 large poblano peppers

- 8 tablespoons shredded pepper jack cheese

- ½ cup full-fat sour cream

Preparation

1- In a medium skillet over medium heat, crumble and brown the sausage powder until no more pink is left. Remove the sausages and drain the fat from the pan. Break the eggs in the pan, scramble and cook until they no longer flow.

2- Place the cooked sausages in a large bowl and stir in the cream cheese. Mix the diced tomatoes and chillies. Gently stir in the eggs.

3- Cut a 4 to 5-inch slit at the top of each poblano, removing the seeds and white membrane with a small knife. Divide the filling into four portions and carefully pour each pepper. Garnish each spoon with 2 tablespoons of pepper jack cheese.

4- Place each pepper in the basket of the air fryer.

5- Set the temperature to 350 ° F and set the timer to 15 minutes.

6- The peppers will be tender and the cheese will be golden when ready. Serve immediately with sour cream.

Nutrition facts per serving

Calories: 489

Fat: 35.6 g

Protein: 22.8 g

Carb: 8.8 g

Fiber: 3.8 g

Cauliflower Avocado Toast

Hands-On Time: **15 minutes**; *Cook Time:* **8 minutes**; *Yield*: **2 servings.**

Ingredients

- 1 (12-ounce) steamer bag cauliflower

- 1 large egg

- ½ cup shredded mozzarella cheese

- 1 ripe medium avocado

- ½ teaspoon garlic powder

- ¼ teaspoon ground black pepper

Preparation

1- Cook the cauliflower according to the directions on the package. Remove from the bag and place in a cheesecloth or a clean towel to remove excess moisture.

2- Place the cauliflower in a large bowl and mix the egg and mozzarella. Cut a piece of parchment to fit it to your air fryer basket. Separate the cauliflower mixture in half and place on the parchment in two mounds. Press the cauliflower mounds into a ¼-inch thick rectangle. Place the parchment in the basket of the air fryer.

3- Set the temperature to 400 ° F and set the timer to 8 minutes.

4- Turn cauliflower halfway through cooking.

5- When the timer rings remove the parchment and let the cauliflower cool for 5 minutes.

6- Open the lawyer and remove the kernel. Pick up the inside, place it in a medium bowl and crush it with garlic powder and pepper. Spread on cauliflower. Serve immediately.

Nutrition facts per serving

Calories: 278

Fat: 15.6 g

Protein: 14.1 g

Carb: 15.9 g

Fiber: 8.2 g

__Hard-Boiled Eggs__

Hands-On Time: **2 minutes**; *Cook Time:* **18 minutes**; *Yield*: **4 servings.**

Ingredients

• 4 large eggs

• 1 cup water

Preparation

1- Place the eggs in a 4-cup round dish and pour water over the eggs. Place the dish in the basket of the fryer.

2- Set the temperature to 300 ° F and set the timer to 18 minutes.

3- Keep the eggs cooked in the refrigerator until they are ready for use or peel them and eat them warm.

Nutrition facts per serving

Calories: 77

Fat: 4.4 g

Protein: 6.3 g

Carb: 0.6 g

Fiber: 0 g

Scrambled Eggs

Hands-On Time: **5 minutes**; *Cook Time:* **15 minutes**; *Yield*: **2 servings.**

Ingredients

• 4 large eggs

• 2 tablespoons unsalted butter, melted

• ½ cup grated cheddar cheese

Preparation

1- Break eggs in a round baking dish and whisk. Place the dish in the basket of the fryer.

2- Set the temperature to 400 ° F and set the timer to 10 minutes.

3- After 5 minutes, mix the eggs and add the butter and cheese. Cook another 3 minutes and stir again.

4- Let the eggs finish cooking an additional 2 minutes or remove them if you like.

5- Use a fork to fluff. Serve hot.

Nutrition facts per serving

Calories: 359

Fat: 27.6 g

Protein: 19.5 g

Carb: 1.1 g

Fiber: 0 g

Cinnamon Roll Sticks

Hands-On Time: **10 minutes**; *Cook Time:* **7 minutes**; *Yield*: **4 servings.**

Ingredients

• 1 cup shredded mozzarella cheese

• 1 ounce full-fat cream cheese

• ⅓ cup blanched finely ground almond flour

• ½ teaspoon baking soda

• ½ cup granular erythritol divided

• 1 teaspoon vanilla extract

• 1 large egg

• 2 tablespoons unsalted butter, melted

• ½ teaspoon ground cinnamon

• 3 tablespoons powdered erythritol

• 2 teaspoons unsweetened vanilla almond milk

Preparation

1- Place the mozzarella in a large microwave-safe bowl cut the cream cheese into small pieces and place in a bowl. Microwave for 45 seconds.

2- Stir in almond flour, baking soda, ¼-cup granular erythritol and vanilla. Soft dough should form. Microwave blends for another 15 seconds if it becomes too stiff.

3- Stir the egg into the dough using your hands if necessary.

4- Cut out a piece of parchment suitable for your air fryer basket. Press the dough into an 8 × 5-inch rectangle on the parchment and cut into eight sticks.

5- In a small bowl, combine butter, cinnamon and remaining granular erythritol. Apply half of the mixture to the top of the sticks and place in the fryer basket.

6- Set the temperature to 400 ° F and set the timer to 7 minutes.

7- Halfway through the cooking time, turn the sticks over and brush with the remaining butter mixture. Once finished, the sticks should be crisp.

8- In a small bowl, whisk erythritol powder and almond milk powder. Sprinkle with cinnamon sticks. Serve hot.

Nutrition facts per serving: *Calories: 233; Fat: 19 g; Protein: 10.3 g; Carb: 2.2 g; Fiber: 1.2 g*

Breakfast Calzone

Hands-On Time: **15 minutes**; *Cook Time:* **15 minutes**; *Yield*: **4 servings.**

Ingredients

- 1½ cup grated mozzarella cheese
- ½ cup blanched ground almond flour
- 1 oz. whole cream cheese
- 1 big whole egg
- 4 large scrambled eggs
- ½ pound of cooked, crumbled breakfast sausages
- 8 tablespoons grated sweet cheddar cheese

Preparation

1- In a large microwave-safe bowl, add mozzarella, almond flour and cream cheese. Microwave for 1 minute. Stir until the mixture is smooth and forms a ball. Add egg and stir until the dough forms.

2- Place the dough between two sheets of parchment paper and spread out ¼ inch thick. Cut the dough into four rectangles.

3- In a large bowl, combine scrambled eggs and cooked sausages. Spread the mixture evenly in each piece of dough by placing it on the lower half of the rectangle. Sprinkle each with 2 tablespoons of cheddar cheese.

4- Fold the rectangle to cover the egg and meat mixture. Pinch, roll or use a wet fork to close the edges completely.

5- Cut out a piece of parchment suitable for your deep fryer basket and place the calzones on the parchment. Place the parchment in the basket of the air fryer.

6- Set the temperature to 380 ° F and set the timer to 15 minutes.

7- Return the calzones halfway through cooking. Once finished, the calzones must be golden in color. Serve immediately.

Nutrition facts per serving

Calories: 560; Fat: 41.7 g; Protein: 34.5 g; Carb: 4.2 g; Fiber: 1.5 g

Cheesy Cauliflower Hash Browns

Hands-On Time: **20 minutes**; *Cook Time:* **12 minutes**; *Yield*: **4 servings.**

Ingredients

• 1 steamer bag cauliflower (12 oz.)

• 1 large egg

• 1 cup grated cheddar cheese

Preparation

1- Place the bag in the microwave and cook according to the directions on the package. Let cool completely and put the cauliflower in a cloth or kitchen towel and squeeze to remove excess moisture.

2- Crush the cauliflower with a fork and add the egg and cheese.

3- Cut out a piece of parchment suitable for your air fryer basket. Take ¼ of the mixture and form it into a brown patty cake. Place it on the parchment and in the fryer basket, working in batches if necessary.

4- Set the temperature to 400 ° F and set the timer to 12 minutes.

5- Turn the browned potatoes halfway through cooking. Once cooked, they will be golden brown. Serve immediately.

Nutrition facts per serving

Calories: 153

Fat: 9.5 g

Protein: 10 g

Carb: 3 g

Fiber: 1.7 g

Pancake Cake

Hands-On Time: **10 minutes**; *Cook Time:* **7 minutes**; *Yield*: **4 servings.**

Ingredients

- ½ cup blanched finely ground almond flour

- ½ cup powdered erythritol

- ½ teaspoon baking powder

- 2 tablespoons unsalted butter, softened

- 1 large egg

- ½ teaspoon unflavored gelatin

- ½ teaspoon vanilla extract

- ½ teaspoon ground cinnamon

Preparation

1- In a large bowl, mix almond flour, erythritol and baking powder. Add butter, egg, gelatin, vanilla and cinnamon. Pour in 6-inch a round dish.

2- Place the dish in the fryer basket.

3- Set the temperature to 300 ° F and set the timer to 7 minutes.

4- When the cake is completely cooked, a toothpick will come out clean. Cut the cake in four and serve.

Nutrition facts per serving

Calories: 153

Fat: 13.4 g

Protein: 5.4 g

Carb: 1.9 g

Fiber: 1.7 g

Poppy Seed Cake

Hands-On Time: **10 minutes**; *Cook Time:* **14 minutes***; Yield*: **6 servings.**

Ingredients

• 1 cup blanched finely ground almond flour

• ½ cup powdered erythritol

• ½ teaspoon baking powder

• ¼ cup unsalted butter, melted

• ¼ cup unsweetened almond milk

• 2 large eggs

• 1 teaspoon vanilla extract

• 1 medium lemon

• 1 teaspoon poppy seeds

Preparation

1- In a large bowl, mix almond flour, erythritol, baking powder, butter, almond milk, eggs and vanilla.

2- Cut the lemon in half and squeeze the juice into a small bowl, then add it to the dough.

3- Using a fine grater, zest the lemon and add 1-tablespoon zest to the dough and mix. Add the poppy seeds to the dough.

4- Pour the dough into a 6-inch non-stick round cake pan. Place the pan in the basket of the fryer.

5- Set the temperature to 300 ° F and set the timer to 14 minutes.

Once cooked, a toothpick inserted in the center will come out almost clean. The cake will finish cooking and firm as it cools. Serve at room temperature.

Nutrition facts per serving

Calories: 204

Fat: 18.2 g

Protein: 6.3 g

Carb: 2.5 g

Fiber: 2.4 g

Crunchy Granola

Hands-On Time: **10 minutes**; *Cook Time:* **5 minutes**; *Yield*: **6 servings.**

Ingredients

• 2 cups pecans chopped

• 1 cup unsweetened coconut flakes

• 1 cup almond slivers

• ⅓ cup sunflower seeds

• ¼ cup golden flaxseed

• ¼ cup low-carb, sugar-free chocolate chips

• ¼ cup granular erythritol

• 2 tablespoons unsalted butter

• 1 teaspoon ground cinnamon

Preparation

1- In a large bowl, combine all ingredients.

2- Place the mixture in a round baking dish of 4 cups. Place the dish in the basket of the fryer.

3- Set the temperature to 320 ° F and set the timer to 5 minutes.

4- Cool completely before serving.

Nutrition facts per serving

Calories: 617

Fat: 55.8 g

Protein: 10.9 g

Carb: 6.5 g

Fiber: 11.2 g

Jalapeño Popper Egg Cups

Hands-On Time: **10 minutes**; *Cook Time:* **10 minutes**; *Yield*: **2 servings.**

Ingredients

• 4 large eggs

• ¼ cup chopped pickled jalapeños

• 2 ounces full-fat cream cheese

• ½ cup shredded sharp Cheddar cheese

Preparation

1- In a medium bowl, beat the eggs and pour into four silicone muffin cups.

2- In a large microwaveable bowl, place the jalapeños, cream cheese and cheddar cheese. Microwave for 30 seconds and stir. Take a spoonful, about ¼ of the mixture and place it in the center of one of the egg cups. Repeat with the rest of the mixture.

3- Place the egg cups in the fryer basket.

4- Set the temperature to 320 ° F and set the timer to 10 minutes.

5- Serve hot.

Nutrition facts per serving

Calories: 354

Fat: 25.3 g

Protein: 21 g

Carb: 2.1 g

Fiber: 0.2 g

Crispy Southwestern Ham Egg Cups

Hands-On Time: **5 minutes**; *Cook Time:* **12 minutes**; *Yield:* **2 servings.**

Ingredients

• 4 (1-ounce) slices deli ham

• 4 large eggs

• 2 tablespoons full-fat sour cream

• ¼ cup diced green bell pepper

• 2 tablespoons diced red bell pepper

• 2 tablespoons diced white onion

• ½ cup shredded medium Cheddar cheese

Preparation

1- Place a slice of ham in the bottom of four mussels.

2- In a large bowl, whisk the eggs with the sour cream. Stir in green pepper, red pepper and onion.

3- Pour the egg mixture into molds filled with ham. Garnish with cheddar cheese. Place the cups in the basket of the fryer.

4- Adjust the temperature to 320 ° F and set the timer to 12 minutes or until the trays are golden brown.

5- Serve hot.

Nutrition facts per serving

Calories: 382

Fat: 23.6 g

Protein: 29.4 g

Carb: 4.6 g

Fiber: 1.4 g

Veggie Frittata

Hands-On Time: **15 minutes**; *Cook Time:* **12 minutes**; *Yield*: **4 servings.**

Ingredients

• 6 large eggs

• ¼ cup heavy whipping cream

• ½ cup chopped broccoli

• ¼ cup chopped yellow onion

• ¼ cup chopped green bell pepper

Preparation

1- In a large bowl, whisk eggs and heavy whipping cream. Stir in broccoli, onion and pepper.

2- Pour into a 6-inch round baking dish. Place the baking dish in the basket of the air fryer.

3- Set the temperature to 350 ° F and set the timer to 12 minutes.

4- Eggs must be firm and well cooked when the frittata is cooked.

5- Serve hot.

Nutrition facts per serving

Calories: 168

Fat: 11.8 g

Protein: 10.2 g

Carb: 2.5 g

Fiber: 0.6 g

Quick and Easy Bacon Strips

Hands-On Time: **5 minutes**; *Cook Time:* **12 minutes**; *Yield*: **4 servings.**

Ingredients

• 8 slices sugar-free bacon

Preparation

1- Place the bacon strips in the fryer basket.

2- Set the temperature to 400 ° F and set the timer to 12 minutes.

3- After 6 minutes, turn the bacon over and continue cooking.

4- Serve hot.

Nutrition facts per serving

Calories: 88

Fat: 6.2 g

Protein: 5.8 g

Carb: 0.2 g

Fiber: 0 g

Nut Cake

Hands-On Time: **15 minutes**; *Cook Time:* **25 minutes**; *Yield*: **6 servings.**

Ingredients

• 1 cup blanched finely ground almond flour

• ½ cup powdered erythritol

• 2 tablespoons ground golden flaxseed

• 2 teaspoons baking powder

• ½ teaspoon ground cinnamon

• ¼ cup unsalted butter, melted

• 2½ teaspoons banana extract

• 1 teaspoon vanilla extract

• ¼ cup full-fat sour cream

• 2 large eggs

• ¼ cup chopped walnuts

Preparation

1- In a large bowl, combine almond flour, erythritol, flaxseed, baking powder and cinnamon.

2- Stir in butter, banana extract, vanilla extract and sour cream.

3- Add the eggs to the mixture and mix gently until everything is well mixed. Stir in the nuts.

4- Pour into a 6-inch nonstick cake pan and place in the air fryer basket.

5- Set the temperature to 300 ° F and set the timer to 25 minutes.

6- The cake will be golden and a toothpick inserted in the center will come out clean when cooked. Cool completely to avoid crumbling.

Nutrition facts per serving

Calories: 263

Fat: 23.6 g

Protein: 7.6 g

Carb: 3.3 g

Fiber: 3.1 g

<u>Cheesy Bell Pepper Eggs</u>

Hands-On Time: **10 minutes**; *Cook Time:* **15 minutes***; Yield*: **4 servings.**

Ingredients

• 4 green bell peppers

• 3 ounces cooked ham, chopped

• ¼ medium onion, peeled and chopped

• 8 large eggs

• 1 cup mild Cheddar cheese

Preparation

1- Cut the top of each pepper. Remove the seeds and white membranes with a small knife. Place the ham and onion in each pepper.

2- Break two eggs in each pepper. Garnish with ¼ cup of cheese per pepper. Place in the basket of the air fryer.

3- Set the temperature to 390 ° F and set the timer to 15 minutes.

4- Once cooked, the peppers will be tender and the eggs will be firm. Serve immediately.

Nutrition facts per serving

Calories: 314

Fat: 18.6 g

Protein: 24.9 g

Carb: 4.6 g

Fiber: 1.7 g

Loaded Cauliflower Breakfast Bake

Hands-On Time: **15 minutes**; *Cook Time:* **20 minutes**; *Yield:* **4 servings.**

Ingredients

- 6 large eggs
- ¼ cup heavy whipping cream
- 1½ cups chopped cauliflower
- 1 cup shredded medium Cheddar cheese
- 1 medium avocado, peeled and pitted
- 8 tablespoons full-fat sour cream
- 2 scallions, sliced on the bias
- 12 slices sugar-free bacon, cooked and crumbled

Preparation

1- In a medium bowl, whisk together the eggs and cream. Pour into a round baking dish of 4 cups.

2- Add the cauliflower and mix, then garnish with cheddar cheese. Place the dish in the basket of the fryer.

3- Set the temperature to 320 ° F and set the timer to 20 minutes.

4- Once cooked, the eggs will be firm and the cheese golden. Slice into four pieces.

5- Slice the avocado and divide it evenly into pieces. Garnish each piece with 2 tablespoons sour cream, chopped green onions and crumbled bacon.

Nutrition facts per serving

Calories: 512

Fat: 38.3 g

Protein: 27.1 g

Carb: 4.3 g

Fiber: 3.2 g

Bacon, Egg, and Cheese Roll Ups

Hands-On Time: **15 minutes**; *Cook Time:* **15 minutes**; *Yield*: **4 servings.**

Ingredients

• 2 tablespoons unsalted butter

• ¼ cup chopped onion

• ½ green bell pepper, seeded and chopped

• 6 large eggs

• 12 slices sugar-free bacon

• 1 cup shredded sharp Cheddar cheese

• ½ cup mild salsa, for dipping

Preparation

1- In a medium skillet over medium heat, melt butter, and add onion, pepper to the pan and sauté for about 3 minutes, until the scents are fragrant and translucent.

2- Whisk the eggs in a small bowl and pour into the pan. Blot eggs with onions and peppers until frothy and well cooked, about 5 minutes. Remove from heat and set aside.

3- On the work surface, place three slices of bacon side by side, overlapping about ¼-inch. Place ¼-cup scrambled eggs in a pile on the side closest to you and sprinkle ¼-cup of cheese on the eggs.

4- Wrap the bacon around the eggs and attach the seam with a toothpick if necessary. Place each roll in the basket of the air fryer.

5- Set the temperature to 350 ° F and set the timer to 15 minutes. Rotate the rolls halfway through cooking.

6- The bacon will be brown and crisp at the end of cooking. Serve immediately with salsa as a dip.

Nutrition facts per serving

Calories: 460

Fat: 31.7 g

Protein: 28.2 g

Carb: 5.3 g

Fiber: 0.8 g

Pumpkin Spice Muffins

Hands-On Time: **10 minutes**; *Cook Time:* **15 minutes**; *Yield*: **6 servings.**

Ingredients

• 1 cup blanched finely ground almond flour

• ½ cup granular erythritol

• ½ teaspoon baking powder

• ¼ cup unsalted butter, softened

• ¼ cup pure pumpkin purée

• ½ teaspoon ground cinnamon

• ¼ teaspoon ground nutmeg

• 1 teaspoon vanilla extract

• 2 large eggs

Preparation

1- In a large bowl, mix almond flour, erythritol, baking powder, butter, pumpkin puree, cinnamon, nutmeg and vanilla.

2- Gently stir in the eggs.

3- Pour the dough evenly into six silicone muffin cups. Place the muffin cups in the basket of the air fryer, working in batches if necessary.

4- Set the temperature to 300 ° F and set the timer to 15 minutes.

5- Once fully cooked, a toothpick inserted in the center will come out almost clean. Serve hot.

Nutrition facts per serving

Calories: 205

Fat: 18 g

Protein: 6.3 g

Carb: 3 g

Fiber: 2.4 g

APPETIZERS AND SNACKS

Sometimes, the appetizers can be more exciting than the meals, and we all ate a plate of delicious bites instead of a meal at least once or twice! This tradition of fun cocktails does not have to end simply because you stick to a low-carb lifestyle. Whether you are hosting an event or looking for a keto version of your favorite restaurant, the recipes in this chapter such as Jalapeno Bacon Roll Packed with Bacon and Cheese and Garlic Bread will keep you satisfied without sabotaging your keto lifestyle!

Garlic Cheese Bread

Hands-On Time: **10 minutes**; *Cook Time:* **10 minutes**; *Yield*: **2 servings**.

Ingredients

- 1 cup shredded mozzarella cheese
- ¼ cup grated Parmesan cheese
- 1 large egg
- ½ teaspoon garlic powder

Preparation

1- Mix all ingredients in a large bowl. Cut a piece of parchment to fit it to your air fryer basket. Press the mixture to form a circle on the parchment and place it in the basket of the air fryer.

2- Set the temperature to 350 ° F and set the timer to 10 minutes.

3- Serve hot.

Nutrition facts per serving

Calories: 258

Fat: 16.6 g

Protein: 19.2 g

Carb: 3.7 g

Fiber: 0.1 g

Crustless 3-Meat Pizza

Hands-On Time: **5 minutes**; *Cook Time:* **5 minutes**; *Yield*: **1 serving**.

Ingredients

• ½ cup shredded mozzarella cheese

• 7 slice pepperoni

• ¼ cup cooked ground sausage

• 2 slices sugar-free bacon, cooked and crumbled

• 1 tablespoon grated Parmesan cheese

• 2 tablespoons low-carb, sugar-free pizza sauce, for dipping

Preparation

1- Cover the bottom of a 6-inch mozzarella cake pan. Place the pepperoni, sausages and bacon on the cheese and sprinkle with Parmesan cheese. Place the pan in the basket of the fryer.

2- Set the temperature to 400 ° F and set the timer to 5 minutes.

3- Remove when the cheese is bubbling and browned. Serve hot with the pizza sauce for dipping.

Nutrition facts per serving

Calories: 466

Fat: 34 g

Protein: 28.1 g

Carb: 4.7 g

Fiber: 0.5 g

Bacon-Wrapped Brie

Hands-On Time: **5 minutes**; *Cook Time:* **10 minutes**; *Yield:* **8 servings**.

Ingredients

• 4 slices sugar-free bacon

• 1 (8-ounce) round Brie

Preparation

1- Place 2 slices of bacon to form an X. Place the third slice of bacon horizontally in the center of the X. Place the fourth slice of bacon vertically on the X. It should look like a plus sign (+) above an X. Then place the brie in the center of the bacon.

2- Wrap the bacon around the brie and fix it with some toothpicks. Cut a piece of parchment paper to fit into your deep fryer basket and place on top of bacon wrapped brie. Place it in the basket of the fryer.

3- Set the temperature to 400 ° F and set the timer to 10 minutes.

4 When 3 minutes remain on the stopwatch, turn the brie gently.

5 Once cooked, the bacon will be crisp and the cheese will be tender and melted. To serve, cut into eight slices.

Nutrition facts per serving

Calories: 116

Fat: 8.9 g

Protein: 7.7 g

Carb: 0.2 g

Fiber: 0 g

Smoky BBQ Roasted Almonds

Hands-On Time: **5 minutes**; *Cook Time:* **6 minutes**; *Yield*: **4 servings**.

Ingredients

- 1 cup raw almonds
- 2 teaspoons coconut oil
- 1 teaspoon chili powder
- ¼ teaspoon cumin
- ¼ teaspoon smoked paprika
- ¼ teaspoon onion powder

Preparation

1- In a large bowl, combine all ingredients until almonds are well coated with oil and spices. Place the almonds in the basket of the air fryer.

2- Set the temperature to 320 ° F and set the timer to 6 minutes.

3- Stir the fryer basket halfway through cooking. Cool completely.

Nutrition facts per serving

Calories: 182

Fat: 16.3 g

Protein: 6.2 g

Carb: 3.3 g

Fiber: 3.3 g

Mozzarella-Stuffed Meatballs

Hands-On Time: **15 minutes**; *Cook Time:* **15 minutes**; *Yield*: **16 meatballs**.

Ingredients

- 1 pound ground beef

- ¼ cup blanched finely ground almond flour

- 1 teaspoon dried parsley

- ½ teaspoon garlic powder

- ¼ teaspoon onion powder

- 1 large egg

- 3 ounces low-moisture, whole-milk mozzarella, cubed

- ½ cup low-carb, no-sugar-added pasta sauce

- ¼ cup grated Parmesan cheese

Preparation

1- In a large bowl, add ground beef, almond flour, parsley, garlic powder, onion powder and egg. Fold the ingredients together until they are completely combined.

2- Form the mixture into 2-inch balls and use your thumb or spoon to create a shrinkage in the center of each dumpling. Place a cheese cube in the center and form the ball around it.

3- Place the meatballs in the air fryer, working in batches if necessary.

4- Set the temperature to 350 ° F and set the timer to 15 minutes.

5- The meatballs will be slightly crispy on the outside and fully cooked when at least 180 ° F inside.

6- When cooking is complete, mix the meatballs with the sauce and sprinkle with grated Parmesan cheese.

Nutrition facts per serving

Calories: 447

Fat: 29.7 g

Protein: 29.6 g

Carb: 3.6 g

Fiber: 1.8 g

Bacon Cheeseburger Dip

Hands-On Time: **20 minutes**; *Cook Time:* **10 minutes**; *Yield:* **6 servings**.

Ingredients

- 8 ounces full-fat cream cheese

- ¼ cup full-fat mayonnaise

- ¼ cup full-fat sour cream

- ¼ cup chopped onion

- 1 teaspoon garlic powder

- 1 tablespoon Worcestershire sauce

- 1¼ cups shredded medium Cheddar cheese, divided

- ½ pound cooked ground beef

- 6 slices sugar-free bacon, cooked and crumbled

- 2 large pickle spears chopped

Preparation

1- Place the cream cheese in a large microwaveable bowl and microwave for 45 seconds. Stir in mayonnaise, sour cream, onion, garlic powder, Worcestershire sauce and 1-cup cheddar cheese. Add cooked ground beef and bacon. Sprinkle remaining cheddar on top.

2- Place in a 6-inch bowl and place it in the basket of the air fryer.

3- Set the temperature to 400 ° F and set the timer to 10 minutes.

4- Soaking is done when the top is golden and bubbling. Sprinkle the pickles on the dish. Serve hot.

Nutrition facts per serving

Calories: 457

Fat: 35 g

Protein: 21.6 g

Carb: 3.6 g

Fiber: 0.2 g

Pizza Rolls

Hands-On Time: **15 minutes**; *Cook Time:* **10 minutes**; *Yield*: **24 rolls**.

Ingredients

• 2 cups shredded mozzarella cheese

• ½ cup almond flour

• 2 large eggs

• 72 slice pepperoni

• 8 (1-ounce) mozzarella string cheese sticks, cut into 3 pieces each

• 2 tablespoons unsalted butter, melted

• ¼ teaspoon garlic powder

• ½ teaspoon dried parsley

• 2 tablespoons grated Parmesan cheese

Preparation

1- In a large microwave-safe bowl, strain the almond and mozzarella flour. Microwave for 1 minute. Remove the bowl and mix until you have a ball of dough. Additional microwaves 30 seconds if necessary.

2- Break the eggs in the bowl and mix until you have a ball of dough. Then wet your hands with water and knead the dough briefly.

3- Cut two large pieces of parchment paper and spray one side of each with a nonstick cooking spray. Place the dough ball between the two sheets, with the sides sprayed against the dough. Use a rolling pin to spread the dough about ¼ inch thick.

4- Use a knife to slice into 24 rectangles. On each rectangle, place 3 slices of pepperoni and 1 piece of cheese in string.

5- Fold the rectangle in half, covering the pepperoni and cheese filling. Pinch or roll the closed sides. Cut a piece of parchment suitable for your air fryer basket and place it in the basket. Place the rolls on the parchment.

6- Set the temperature to 350 ° F and set the timer to 10 minutes.

7- After 5 minutes, open the fryer and turn over the pizza rolls. Restart the fryer and continue cooking until the pizza buns are golden brown.

8- In a small bowl, remove the butter, garlic powder and parsley. Brush the mixture with baked bread and sprinkle with Parmesan cheese.

9- Serve hot.

Nutrition facts per serving

Calories: 333

Fat: 24 g

Protein: 20.7 g

Carb: 2.5 g

Fiber: 0.8 g

Beef Jerky

Hands-On Time: **5 minutes**; *Cook Time:* **4 hours**; *Yield*: **10 servings**.

Ingredients

• 1 pound flat iron beef, thinly sliced

• ¼ cup soy sauce

• 2 teaspoons Worcestershire sauce

• ¼ teaspoon crushed red pepper flakes

• ¼ teaspoon garlic powder

• ¼ teaspoon onion powder

Preparation

1- Place all ingredients in a plastic bag or covered container and marinate 2 hours in the refrigerator.

2- Place each slice of dried meat on the air fryer grid in a single layer.

3- Set the temperature to 160 ° F and set the timer to 4 hours.

4- Cool and store in an airtight container for up to 1 week.

Nutrition facts per serving

Calories: 85

Fat: 3.5 g

Protein: 10.2 g

Carb: 0.6 g

Fiber: 0 g

Pork Rind Nachos

Hands-On Time: **5 minutes**; *Cook Time:* **5 minutes**; *Yield*: **2 servings**.

Ingredients

- 1 ounce pork rinds

- 4 ounces shredded cooked chicken

- ½ cup shredded Monterey jack cheese

- ¼ cup sliced pickled jalapeños

- ¼ cup guacamole

- ¼ cup full-fat sour cream

Preparation

1- Place the pork rinds in a 6-inch round pan. Cover with grated chicken and Monterey Jack cheese. Place the pan in the basket of the fryer.

2- Set the temperature to 370 ° F and set the timer for 5 minutes or until the cheese is melted.

3- Garnish with jalapeños, guacamole and sour cream. Serve immediately.

Nutrition facts per serving

Calories: 395

Fat: 27.5 g

Protein: 30.1 g

Carb: 1.8 g

Fiber: 1.2 g

Pork Rind Tortillas

Hands-On Time: **10 minutes**; *Cook Time:* **5 minutes**; *Yield*: **4 servings**.

Ingredients

• 1 ounce pork rinds

• ¾ cup shredded mozzarella cheese

• 2 tablespoons full-fat cream cheese

• 1 large egg

Preparation

1- Place the pork rind in the food processor and mix until it is finely ground.

2- Place the mozzarella in a large microwaveable bowl. Then break the cream cheese into small pieces and add to the bowl. Heat in the microwave for 30 seconds or until both cheeses are melted and can be easily mixed into a ball. Add the chopped pork zest and egg to the cheese mixture.

3- Continue stirring until the mixture forms a ball. If it cools too much and the cheese hardens, microwave for another 10 seconds.

4- Separate the dough into four small balls. Place each ball of dough between two sheets of parchment paper and roll into a ¼-inch flat layer.

5- Place the tortillas in the basket of the air fryer in one layer, working in batches if necessary.

6- Set the temperature to 400 ° F and set the timer to 5 minutes.

7- The tortillas will be crisp and firm once cooked. Serve immediately.

Nutrition facts per serving

Calories: 145

Fat: 10 g

Protein: 10.7 g

Carb: 0.8 g

Fiber: 0 g

Ranch Roasted Almonds

Hands-On Time: **5 minutes**; *Cook Time:* **6 minutes**; *Yield*: **2 cups**.

Ingredients

• 2 cups raw almonds

• 2 tablespoons unsalted butter, melted

• ½ (1-ounce) ranch dressing mix packet

Preparation

1- In a large bowl, mix the almonds in the butter to coat them. Sprinkle ranch mixture over almonds and mix. Place the almonds in the basket of the air fryer.

2- Set the temperature to 320 ° F and set the timer to 6 minutes.

3- Shake the basket two or three times while cooking.

4- Cool for at least 20 minutes. The almonds will be soft but will become crispier during cooling.

Nutrition facts per serving

Calories: 190

Fat: 16.7 g

Protein: 6 g

Carb: 4 g

Fiber: 3 g

Mozzarella Sticks

Hands-On Time: **1 hour**; *Cook Time:* **10 minutes**; *Yield*: **12 sticks**.

Ingredients

• 6 (1-ounce) mozzarella string cheese sticks

• ½ cup grated Parmesan cheese

• ½ ounce pork rinds, finely ground

• 1 teaspoon dried parsley

• 2 large eggs

Preparation

1- Place the mozzarella sticks on a cutting board and cut them in half. Freeze for 45 minutes or until firm. In the case of overnight frost, remove the frozen sticks after 1 hour, place them in an airtight zippered storage bag and return to the freezer for future use.

2- In a large bowl, combine Parmesan, chopped pork zest and parsley.

3- In a medium bowl, beat the eggs.

4- Dip a frozen mozzarella stick into the beaten eggs, then into the Parmesan mixture to coat well. Repeat with the remaining sticks. Place the mozzarella sticks in the basket of the air fryer.

5- Set the temperature to 400 ° F and set the timer to 10 minutes or until golden.

6- Serve hot.

Nutrition facts per serving

Calories: 236

Fat: 13.8 g

Protein: 19.2 g

Carb: 4.7 g

Fiber: 0 g

Bacon-Wrapped Onion Rings

Hands-On Time: **5 minutes**; *Cook Time:* **10 minutes**; *Yield*: **4 servings**.

Ingredients

• 1 large onion, peeled

• 1 tablespoon sriracha

• 8 slices sugar-free bacon

Preparation

1- Slice the onion into quarters of ¼-inch thick. Brush the onion slices with the sriracha. Take two slices of onion and roll the bacon around the pucks. Repeat with the rest of the onion and bacon. Place in the basket of the air fryer.

2- Set the temperature to 350 ° F and set the timer to 10 minutes.

3- Use tongs to turn onion rings halfway through cooking. Once cooked, the bacon will be crisp.

4- Serve hot.

Nutrition facts per serving

Calories: 105

Fat: 5.9 g

Protein: 7.5 g

Carb: 3.7 g

Fiber: 0.6 g

<u>Mozzarella Pizza Crust</u>

Hands-On Time: **5 minutes**; *Cook Time:* **10 minutes**; *Yield*: **1 serving**.

Ingredients

• ½ cup shredded whole-milk mozzarella cheese

• 2 tablespoons blanched finely ground almond flour

• 1 tablespoon full-fat cream cheese

• 1 large egg white

Preparation

1- Place the mozzarella, almond flour and cream cheese in a microwaveable bowl. Microwave for 30 seconds. Stir until you have a smooth ball of dough, then add the egg white and stir until a round and soft dough forms.

2- Squeeze into a 6-inch round pizza crust.

3- Cut a piece of parchment into the basket of your air fryer and place the crust on the parchment. Place in the basket of the air fryer.

4- Set the temperature to 350 ° F and set the timer to 10 minutes.

5- Turn over after 5 minutes and then place the desired fillings on the crust. Continue cooking until golden. Serve immediately.

Nutrition facts per serving

Calories: 314

Fat: 22.7 g

Protein: 19.9 g

Carb: 3.6 g

Fiber: 1.5 g

Spicy Buffalo Chicken Dip

Hands-On Time: **10 minutes**; *Cook Time:* **10 minutes**; *Yield*: **4 servings**.

Ingredients

- 1 cup cooked, diced chicken breast

- 8 ounces full-fat cream cheese, softened

- ½ cup buffalo sauce

- ⅓ cup full-fat ranch dressing

- ⅓ cup chopped pickled jalapeños

- 1½ cups shredded medium Cheddar cheese, divided

- 2 scallions, sliced on the bias

Preparation

1- Place the chicken in a large bowl. Add cream cheese, buffalo sauce and ranch vinaigrette. Stir until the sauces are well mixed and especially smooth. Stir in the jalapeños and 1-cup cheddar cheese.

2- Pour the mixture into a 4-cup baking dish and place the rest of the cheddar on top. Place the dish in the basket of the fryer.

3- Set the temperature to 350 ° F and set the timer to 10 minutes.

4- Once finished, the top will be brown and the dip bubbling. Garnish with chopped shallots. Serve hot.

Nutrition facts per serving

Calories: 472

Fat: 32 g

Protein: 25.6 g

Carb: 8.5 g

Fiber: 0.6 g

Garlic Parmesan Chicken Wings

Hands-On Time: **5 minutes**; *Cook Time:* **25 minutes**; *Yield*: **4 servings**.

Ingredients

• 2 pounds raw chicken wings

• 1 teaspoon pink Himalayan salt

• ½ teaspoon garlic powder

• 1 tablespoon baking powder

• 4 tablespoons unsalted butter, melted

• ⅓ cup grated Parmesan cheese

• ¼ teaspoon dried parsley

Preparation

1- In a large bowl, place chicken wings, salt, ½ teaspoon garlic powder and baking powder, then mix. Place the wings in the basket of the fryer.

2- Set the temperature to 400 ° F and set the timer to 25 minutes.

3- Stir the basket two or three times during cooking.

4- In a small bowl, combine butter, Parmesan and parsley.

5- Remove the wings from the fryer and place in a large, clean bowl. Pour the butter mixture on the wings and mix until well coated. Serve hot.

Nutrition facts per serving

Calories: 565

Fat: 42.1 g

Protein: 41.8 g

Carb: 2.1 g

Fiber: 0.1 g

Spicy Spinach Artichoke Dip

Hands-On Time: **10 minutes**; *Cook Time:* **10 minutes**; *Yield*: **6 servings**.

Ingredients

- 10 ounces frozen spinach, drained and thawed

- 1 can artichoke (14-ounce), drained and chopped

- ¼ cup chopped pickled jalapeños

- 8 ounces full-fat cream cheese, softened

- ¼ cup full-fat mayonnaise

- ¼ cup full-fat sour cream

- ½ teaspoon garlic powder

- ¼ cup grated Parmesan cheese

- 1 cup shredded pepper jack cheese

Preparation

1- Mix all ingredients in a 4-cup baking bowl. Place in the basket of the air fryer.

2- Set the temperature to 320 ° F and set the timer to 10 minutes.

3- Remove when brown and bubbling. Serve hot.

Nutrition facts per serving

Calories: 226

Fat: 15.9 g

Protein: 10 g

Carb: 6.5 g

Fiber: 3.7 g

Bacon Jalapeño Cheese Bread

Hands-On Time: **10 minutes**; *Cook Time:* **15 minutes**; *Yield*: **8 sticks**.

Ingredients

• 2 cups shredded mozzarella cheese

• ¼ cup grated Parmesan cheese

• ¼ cup chopped pickled jalapeños

• 2 large eggs

• 4 slices sugar-free bacon, cooked and chopped

Preparation

1- Mix all ingredients in a large bowl. Cut a piece of parchment to fit it to your air fryer basket.

2- Moisten your hands with a little water and squeeze the mixture into a circle. You may need to separate this into two small cheeses, depending on the size of your fryer.

3- Place parchment bread and cheese bread in the basket of the air fryer.

4- Set the temperature to 320 ° F and set the timer to 15 minutes.

5- Gently turn the bread over when there are only 5 minutes left.

6- Once cooked, the top will be golden. Serve hot.

Nutrition facts per serving

Calories: 273

Fat: 18.1 g

Protein: 20.1 g

Carb: 2.1 g

Fiber: 0.1 g

Bacon-Wrapped Jalapeño Poppers

Hands-On Time: **15 minutes**; *Cook Time:* **12 minutes**; *Yield*: **4 servings**.

Ingredients

• 6 jalapeños (about 4-inch long each)

• 3 ounces full-fat cream cheese

• ⅓ cup shredded medium Cheddar cheese

• ¼ teaspoon garlic powder

• 12 slices sugar-free bacon

Preparation

1- Cut the top of the jalapeños and cut the center in half lengthwise. Use a knife to gently remove the white membrane and pepper seeds.

2- In a large microwave-safe bowl, strain the cream cheese, cheddar and garlic powder. Microwave for 30 seconds and stir. Place the cheese mixture in hollow jalapeños.

3- Wrap a slice of bacon around each half of the jalapeño, covering the pepper completely. Place in the basket of the air fryer.

4- Set the temperature to 400 ° F and set the timer to 12 minutes.

5- Turn the peppers halfway through cooking. Serve hot.

Nutrition facts per serving

Calories: 246

Fat: 17.9 g

Protein: 14.4 g

Carb: 2 g

Fiber: 0.6 g

Prosciutto-Wrapped Parmesan Asparagus

Hands-On Time: **10 minutes**; *Cook Time:* **10 minutes**; *Yield*: **4 servings**.

Ingredients

- 1 pound asparagus

- 12 (0.5-ounce) slices prosciutto

- 1 tablespoon coconut oil, melted

- 2 teaspoons lemon juice

- ⅛ teaspoon red pepper flakes

- ⅓ cup grated Parmesan cheese

- 2 tablespoons salted butter, melted

Preparation

1- On a clean work surface, place an asparagus spear on a slice of prosciutto.

2- Sprinkle with coconut oil and lemon juice. Sprinkle asparagus flakes with red pepper and Parmesan cheese. Roll the prosciutto around the asparagus spear. Place in the basket of the air fryer.

3- Set the temperature to 375 ° F and set the timer to 10 minutes.

4- Sprinkle the bread with butter asparagus before serving.

Nutrition facts per serving

Calories: 263

Fat: 20.2 g

Protein: 13.9 g

Carb: 4.3 g

Fiber: 2.4 g

Mini Sweet Pepper Poppers

Hands-On Time: **15 minutes**; *Cook Time:* **8 minutes**; *Yield*: **16 halves**.

Ingredients

• 8 mini sweet peppers

• 4 ounces full-fat cream cheese, softened

• 4 slices sugar-free bacon, cooked and crumbled

• ¼ cup shredded pepper jack cheese

Preparation

1- Remove the top of the peppers and cut them in half lengthwise.

2- In a small bowl, combine the cream cheese, bacon and pepper.

3- Put 3 teaspoons of mixture in each pepper and squeeze gently. Place in the basket of the fryer.

4- Set the temperature to 400 ° F and set the timer to 8 minutes.

5- Serve hot.

Nutrition facts per serving

Calories: 176

Fat: 13.4 g

Protein: 7.4 g

Carb: 2.7 g

Fiber: 0.9 g

SIDE DISHES

Accompaniments can often be one of the most difficult foods to find to complete a convivial meal. Traditional white rice or macaroni and cheese can be easy to combine, but once you have started your low carb lifestyle, these dishes are no longer your friends. Carbohydrates in many traditional side dishes can leave you feeling heavy and will certainly prevent you from getting ketosis. Fortunately, your air fryer can help you prepare quickly and easily without having to light your oven. This chapter will show you how to prepare recipes such as sausage stuffed mushroom caps and cheese cauliflower broths that will spark a revolution!

Dinner Rolls

Hands-On Time: **10 minutes**; *Cook Time:* **12 minutes**; *Yield:* **6 servings**.

Ingredients

- 1 cup shredded mozzarella cheese
- 1 ounce full-fat cream cheese
- 1 cup blanched finely ground almond flour
- ¼ cup ground flaxseed
- ½ teaspoon baking powder
- 1 large egg

Preparation

1- Place the mozzarella, cream cheese and almond flour in a large microwaveable bowl. Microwave for 1 minute. Mix until smooth.

2- Add flaxseed, baking powder and egg until well blended and smooth. Microwave 15 seconds more if it becomes too firm.

3- Divide the dough into six pieces and roll into balls. Place the balls in the basket of the air fryer.

4- Set the temperature to 320 ° F and set the timer to 12 minutes.

5- Allow the rollers to cool completely before serving.

Nutrition facts per serving

Calories: 228

Fat: 18.1 g

Protein: 10.8 g

Carb: 2.9 g

Fiber: 3.9 g

Avocado Fries

Hands-On Time: **15 minutes**; *Cook Time:* **5 minutes**; *Yield*: **4 servings**.

Ingredients

• 2 medium avocados

• 1 ounce pork rinds, finely ground

Preparation

1- Cut each lawyer in half. Remove the pit. Carefully remove the skin and cut the flesh into ¼-inch-thick slices.

2- Place the pork rinds in a medium bowl and squeeze each piece of avocado into the pork rinds to coat. Place the avocado pieces in the basket of the fryer.

3- Set the temperature to 350 ° F and set the timer to 5 minutes.

4- Serve immediately.

Nutrition facts per serving

Calories: 153

Fat: 11.9 g

Protein: 5.4 g

Carb: 1.3 g

Fiber: 11.9 g

Roasted Eggplant

Hands-On Time: **15 minutes**; *Cook Time:* **15 minutes**; *Yield*: **4 servings**.

Ingredients

- 1 large eggplant
- 2 tablespoons olive oil
- ¼ teaspoon salt
- ½ teaspoon garlic powder

Preparation

1- Remove top and bottom of the eggplant. Slice eggplant into round slices ¼-inch thick.

2- Brush the slices with olive oil. Sprinkle with salt and garlic powder. Place the eggplant slices in the basket of the air fryer.

3- Set the temperature to 390 ° F and set the timer to 15 minutes.

4- Serve immediately.

Nutrition facts per serving

Calories: 91

Fat: 6.7 g

Protein: 1.3 g

Carb: 3.8 g

Fiber: 3.7 g

Pita-Style Chips

Hands-On Time: **10 minutes**; *Cook Time:* **5 minutes**; *Yield*: **4 servings**.

Ingredients

- 1 cup shredded mozzarella cheese

- ½ ounce pork rinds, finely ground

- ¼ cup blanched finely ground almond flour

- 1 large egg

Preparation

1- Place the mozzarella in a large microwaveable bowl and microwave for 30 seconds or until melted. Add the rest of the ingredients and stir until an almost smooth paste form easily into a ball. If the dough is too hard, microwave for 15 seconds.

2- Roll the dough between two pieces of parchment in a large rectangle, then use a knife to cut the shavings into a triangle shape. Place the fries in the basket of the fryer.

3- Set the temperature to 350 ° F and set the timer to 5 minutes.

4- The chips will be golden and firm when finished. As they cool, they will become even firmer.

Nutrition facts per serving

Calories: 161

Fat: 11.6 g

Protein: 11.3 g

Carb: 1.4 g

Fiber: 0.8 g

Fried Pickles

Hands-On Time: **10 minutes**; *Cook Time:* **5 minutes**; *Yield*: **4 servings**.

Ingredients

- 1 tablespoon coconut flour
- ⅓ cup blanched finely ground almond flour
- 1 teaspoon chili powder
- ¼ teaspoon garlic powder
- 1 large egg
- 1 cup sliced pickles

Preparation

1- In a medium bowl, whisk together the coconut flour, almond flour, chili powder and garlic powder.

2- Whip the egg in a small bowl.

3- Tap each pickle with a paper towel and dive into the egg. Then flirt in the flour mixture. Place the pickles in the basket of the fryer.

4- Set the temperature to 400 ° F and set the timer to 5 minutes.

5- Turn the gherkins halfway through cooking.

Nutrition facts per serving

Calories: 85

Fat: 6.1 g

Protein: 4.3 g

Carb: 2.3 g

Fiber: 2.3 g

Roasted Garlic

Hands-On Time: **5 minutes**; *Cook Time:* **20 minutes**; *Yield*: **12 servings**.

Ingredients

- 1 medium head garlic

- 2 teaspoons avocado oil

Preparation

1- Remove any excess skin from the garlic but leave the pods covered. Cut ¼ of the garlic head, exposing the end of the pods.

2- Sprinkle with avocado oil. Place the garlic head in a small sheet of aluminum foil, wrapping it completely. Place it in the basket of the fryer.

3- Set the temperature to 400 ° F and set the timer to 20 minutes. If your head of garlic is a little smaller, check it after 15 minutes.

4- Once finished, the garlic should be golden brown and very soft.

5- To serve, the cloves should come out and be easily spread or sliced.

Nutrition facts per serving

Calories: 11

Fat: 0.1 g

Protein: 0.2 g

Carb: 0.9 g

Fiber: 0.1 g

Kale Chips

Hands-On Time: **5 minutes**; *Cook Time:* **5 minutes**; *Yield*: **4 servings**.

Ingredients

• 4 cups stemmed kale

• 2 teaspoons avocado oil

• ½ teaspoon salt

Preparation

1- In a large bowl, combine kale with avocado oil and sprinkle with salt. Place in the basket of the air fryer.

2- Set the temperature to 400 ° F and set the timer to 5 minutes.

3- Kale will be crisp when finished. Serve immediately.

Nutrition facts per serving

Calories: 25

Fat: 2.2 g

Protein: 0.5 g

Carb: 0.7 g

Fiber: 0.4 g

Flatbread

Hands-On Time: **5 minutes**; *Cook Time:* **7 minutes**; *Yield:* **2 servings**.

Ingredients

- 1 cup shredded mozzarella cheese

- ¼ cup blanched finely ground almond flour

- 1 ounce full-fat cream cheese, softened

Preparation

1- In a large microwave-safe bowl, melt the mozzarella in the microwave for 30 seconds. Stir in almond flour until smooth, then add cream cheese. Continue mixing until the dough forms, gently kneading it with wet hands if necessary.

2- Divide the dough into two pieces and spread ¼-inch thick between two pieces of parchment paper and cut another piece of baking paper to fit your air fryer basket.

3- Place a piece of flatbread on your parchment and in the air fryer, working twice as necessary.

4- Set the temperature to 320 ° F and set the timer to 7 minutes.

5- Halfway through cooking, turn over the flatbread. Serve hot.

Nutrition facts per serving

Calories: 296

Fat: 22.6 g

Protein: 16.3 g

Carb: 3.3 g

Fiber: 1.5 g

Radish Chips

Hands-On Time: **10 minutes**; *Cook Time:* **5 minutes**; *Yield*: **4 servings**.

Ingredients

- 2 cups water

- 1 pound radishes

- ¼ teaspoon onion powder

- ¼ teaspoon paprika

- ½ teaspoon garlic powder

- 2 tablespoons coconut oil, melted

Preparation

1- Place the water in a medium saucepan and bring to the boil on the stove.

2- Remove the top and bottom of each radish, then use a mandolin to cut into thin, even slices. You can also use the slicing blade in the food processor for this step.

3- Place the radish slices in boiling water for 5 minutes or until they become translucent. Remove them from the water and place them in a clean towel to absorb excess moisture.

4- Mix the radish chips in a large bowl with the rest of the ingredients until they are completely coated with oil and seasoning. Place the radish chips in the basket of the fryer.

5- Set the temperature to 320 ° F and set the timer to 5 minutes.

6- Shake the basket two or three times during cooking. Serve hot.

Nutrition facts per serving

Calories: 77

Fat: 6.5 g

Protein: 0.8 g

Carb: 2.2 g

Fiber: 1.8 g

Loaded Roasted Broccoli

Hands-On Time: **10 minutes**; *Cook Time:* **10 minutes**; *Yield*: **2 servings**.

Ingredients

• 3 cups fresh broccoli florets

• 1 tablespoon coconut oil

• ½ cup shredded sharp Cheddar cheese

• ¼ cup full-fat sour cream

• 4 slices sugar-free bacon, cooked and crumbled

• 1 scallion sliced on the bias

Preparation

1- Place the broccoli in the basket of the air fryer and sprinkle with coconut oil.

2- Set the temperature to 350 ° F and set the timer to 10 minutes.

3- Stir the basket two or three times during cooking to avoid burns.

4- When broccoli begins to bite at the ends, remove it from the fryer. Garnish with grated cheese, sour cream and crumbled bacon and garnish with shallot slices.

Nutrition facts per serving

Calories: 361

Fat: 25.7 g

Protein: 18.4 g

Carb: 6.9 g

Fiber: 3.6 g

Zucchini Parmesan Chips

Hands-On Time: **10 minutes**; *Cook Time:* **10 minutes**; *Yield*: **4 servings**.

Ingredients

• 2 medium zucchini

• 1 ounce pork rinds

• ½ cup grated Parmesan cheese

• 1 large egg

Preparation

1- Cut zucchini into ¼-inch slices. Place it between two layers of paper towels or a clean towel for 30 minutes to remove excess moisture.

2- Place the pork rinds in the food processor and mix until they are ground. Pour into a medium bowl and mix with Parmesan cheese.

3- Beat the egg in a small bowl.

4- Dip the zucchini slices in the egg and then into the pork rind mixture, coating them as completely as possible. Carefully place each slice in the basket of the air fryer in one layer, working in batches if necessary.

5- Set the temperature to 320 ° F and set the timer to 10 minutes.

6- Sauté fries halfway through cooking. Serve hot.

Nutrition facts per serving

Calories: 121

Fat: 6.7 g

Protein: 9.9 g

Carb: 3.2 g

Fiber: 0.6 g

Buffalo Cauliflower

Hands-On Time: **5 minutes**; *Cook Time:* **5 minutes**; *Yield*: **4 servings**.

Ingredients

• 4 cup cauliflower florets

• 2 tablespoons salted butter, melted

• ½ (1-ounce) dry ranch seasoning packet

• ¼ cup buffalo sauce

Preparation

1- In a large bowl, combine cauliflower with butter and ranch. Place in the basket of the air fryer.

2- Set the temperature to 400 ° F and set the timer to 5 minutes.

3- Shake the basket two or three times while cooking. Once tender, remove the cauliflower from the deep fryer basket and mix with buffalo sauce. Serve hot.

Nutrition facts per serving

Calories: 87

Fat: 5.6 g

Protein: 2.1 g

Carb: 5.2 g

Fiber: 2.1 g

Green Bean Casserole

Hands-On Time: **10 minutes**; *Cook Time:* **15 minutes**; *Yield*: **4 servings**.

Ingredients

• 4 tablespoons unsalted butter

• ¼ cup diced yellow onion

• ½ cup chopped white mushrooms

• ½ cup heavy whipping cream

• 1 ounce full-fat cream cheese

• ½ cup chicken broth

• ¼ teaspoon xanthan gum

• 1 pound fresh green beans, edges trimmed

• ½ ounce pork rinds, finely ground

Preparation

1- In a medium skillet over medium heat, melt butter; Sauté the onions and mushrooms until they become tender and fragrant, about 3 to 5 minutes.

2- Add the heavy whipping cream, cream cheese and broth to the pan. Whisk until smooth. Bring to a boil then reduce to a low heat; Sprinkle xanthan gum into the pan and remove from heat.

3- Cut the green beans into 2-inch pieces and place in a 4-cup baking dish. Pour the sauce mixture over them and stir until they are well coated. Garnish the dish with chopped pork rind. Place in the basket of the air fryer.

4- Set the temperature to 320 ° F and set the timer to 15 minutes.

The top will be tender with a fork of green beans and golden once cooked. Serve hot.

Nutrition facts per serving

Calories: 267

Fat: 23.4 g

Protein: 3.6 g

Carb: 6.5 g

Fiber: 3.2 g

Cilantro Lime Roasted Cauliflower

Hands-On Time: **10 minutes**; *Cook Time:* **7 minutes**; *Yield*: **4 servings**.

Ingredients

• 2 cups chopped cauliflower florets

• 2 tablespoons coconut oil, melted

• 2 teaspoon chili powder

• ½ teaspoon garlic powder

• 1 medium lime

• 2 tablespoons chopped cilantro

Preparation

1- In a large bowl, combine the cauliflower with the coconut oil. Sprinkle with chili powder and garlic. Place the seasoned cauliflower in the basket of the air fryer.

2- Set the temperature to 350 ° F and set the timer to 7 minutes.

3- The cauliflower will be tender and begin to turn golden. Place in a serving bowl.

4- Cut the lime into quarters and squeeze the cauliflower juice. Garnish with coriander.

Nutrition facts per serving

Calories: 73

Fat: 6.5 g

Protein: 1.1 g

Carb: 2.2 g

Fiber: 1.1 g

Coconut Flour Cheesy Garlic Biscuits

Hands-On Time: **10 minutes**; *Cook Time:* **12 minutes**; *Yield*: **4 servings**.

Ingredients

- ⅓ cup coconut flour
- ½ teaspoon baking powder
- ½ teaspoon garlic powder
- 1 large egg
- ¼ cup unsalted butter, melted and divided
- ½ cup shredded sharp Cheddar cheese
- 1 scallion sliced

Preparation

1- In a large bowl, combine the coconut flour, baking powder and garlic powder.

2- Stir in egg, half the melted butter, cheddar cheese and green onions. Pour the mixture into a 6-inch round pan. Place in the basket of the air fryer.

3- Set the temperature to 320 ° F and set the timer to 12 minutes.

4- To serve, remove from pan and let cool completely. Slice into four pieces and pour remaining melted butter over each.

Nutrition facts per serving

Calories: 218

Fat: 16.9 g

Protein: 7.2 g

Carb: 3.4 g

Fiber: 3.4 g

Crispy Brussels Sprouts

Hands-On Time: **5 minutes**; *Cook Time:* **10 minutes**; *Yield*: **4 servings**.

Ingredients

• 1 pound Brussels sprouts

• 1 tablespoon coconut oil

• 1 tablespoon unsalted butter, melted

Preparation

1- Remove all the loose leaves from the Brussels sprouts and cut them in half.

2- Sprinkle the coconut oil sprouts and place them in the deep fryer basket.

3- Set the temperature to 400 ° F and set the timer to 10 minutes. You may want to mix gently halfway through, depending on how they start to brown.

4- When fully cooked, they should be tender with darker caramelized spots. Remove from the basket of the deep fryer and drizzle with melted butter. Serve immediately.

Nutrition facts per serving

Calories: 90

Fat: 6.1 g

Protein: 2.9 g

Carb: 4.3 g

Fiber: 3.2 g

Cheesy Cauliflower Tots

Hands-On Time: **15 minutes**; *Cook Time:* **12 minutes**; *Yield*: **16 tots**.

Ingredients

- 1 large head cauliflower

- 1 cup shredded mozzarella cheese

- ½ cup grated Parmesan cheese

- 1 large egg

- ¼ teaspoon garlic powder

- ¼ teaspoon dried parsley

- ⅛ teaspoon onion powder

Preparation

1- On the stove, fill a large saucepan with 2 cups of water and place a damper in the pan. Bring the water to a boil. Cut the cauliflower into florets and place it on the steamer basket. Cover the pot with a lid.

2- Steam the cauliflower for 7 minutes until tender. Remove from the steam basket and place in a cheesecloth or a clean cloth and let cool. Squeeze the sink to remove as much excess moisture as possible. The mixture will be too soft to form tots if all moisture is removed. Crush with a fork until smooth.

3- Put the cauliflower in a large bowl and add the mozzarella, Parmesan, egg, garlic powder, parsley and onion powder. Stir until completely combined. The mixture should be moist but easy to mold.

4- Take 2 tablespoons of the mixture and roll into shape. Repeat with the rest of the mixture. Place in the basket of the air fryer.

5- Set the temperature to 320 ° F and set the timer to 12 minutes.

6- Turn around halfway through cooking. Cauliflowers should be browned at the end of cooking. Serve hot.

Nutrition facts per serving

Calories: 181

Fat: 9.5 g

Protein: 13.5 g

Carb: 6.6 g

Fiber: 3 g

Fried Green Tomatoes

Hands-On Time: **10 minutes**; *Cook Time:* **7 minutes**; *Yield*: **4 servings**.

Ingredients

• 2 medium green tomatoes

• 1 large egg

• ¼ cup blanched finely ground almond flour

• ⅓ cup grated Parmesan cheese

Preparation

1- Cut the tomatoes into ½-inch slices. In a medium bowl, whisk the egg. In a large bowl, combine almond flour and Parmesan cheese.

2- Dip each slice of tomato in the egg, then slides it into the almond flour mixture; Place the slices in the basket of the air fryer.

3- Set the temperature to 400 ° F and set the timer to 7 minutes.

4- Turn the slices halfway through cooking. Serve immediately.

Nutrition facts per serving

Calories: 106

Fat: 6.7 g

Protein: 6.2 g

Carb: 4.5 g

Fiber: 1.4 g

Jicama Fries

Hands-On Time: **10 minutes**; *Cook Time:* **20 minutes**; *Yield*: **4 servings**.

Ingredients

- 1 small jicama peeled
- ¾ teaspoon chili powder
- ¼ teaspoon garlic powder
- ¼ teaspoon onion powder
- ¼ teaspoon ground black pepper

Preparation

1- Cut the jicama into matches.

2- Place the pieces in a small bowl and sprinkle with the rest of the ingredients. Place the fries in the basket of the fryer.

3- Set the temperature to 350 ° F and set the timer to 20 minutes.

4- Stir the basket two or three times during cooking. Serve hot.

Nutrition facts per serving

Calories: 37

Fat: 0.1 g

Protein: 0.8 g

Carb: 4 g

Fiber: 4.7 g

Quick and Easy Home Fries

Hands-On Time: **10 minutes**; *Cook Time:* **10 minutes**; *Yield*: **4 servings**.

Ingredients

- 1 medium jicama peeled
- 1 tablespoon coconut oil, melted
- ¼ teaspoon ground black pepper
- ½ teaspoon pink Himalayan salt
- 1 green bell pepper seeded and diced
- ½ medium white onion, peeled and diced

Preparation

1- Cut the jicama into 1-inch cubes. Place in a large bowl and mix with coconut oil until well coated. Sprinkle with pepper and salt. Place in the basket of air fryer with peppers and onion.

2- Set the temperature to 400 ° F and set the timer to 10 minutes.

3- Shake two or three times while cooking. The jicama will be soft and dark around the edges. Serve immediately.

Nutrition facts per serving

Calories: 97

Fat: 3.3 g

Protein: 1.5 g

Carb: 7.8 g

Fiber: 8 g

Parmesan Herb Focaccia Bread

Hands-On Time: **10 minutes**; *Cook Time:* **10 minutes**; *Yield*: **6 servings**.

Ingredients

• 1 cup shredded mozzarella cheese

• 1 ounce full-fat cream cheese

• 1 cup blanched finely ground almond flour

• ¼ cup ground golden flaxseed

• ¼ cup grated Parmesan cheese

• ½ teaspoon baking soda

• 2 large eggs

• ½ teaspoon garlic powder

• ¼ teaspoon dried basil

• ¼ teaspoon dried rosemary

• 2 tablespoons salted butter, melted and divided

Preparation

1- Place the mozzarella, cream cheese and almond flour in a large microwaveable bowl and leave in the microwave for 1 minute. Add the flaxseed, Parmesan and baking soda and stir until the bale forms well. If the mixture cools too much, it will be difficult to mix. Microwave for 10–15 seconds to warm if necessary.

2- Stir in the eggs. You may need to use your hands to incorporate them completely. Just keep stirring and they will absorb into the dough.

3- Sprinkle the dough with garlic powder, basil and rosemary and knead to form a paste. Grease a 6-inch round pan with 1 tablespoon of melted butter. Press the dough evenly into the mold. Place the pan in the basket of the fryer.

4- Set the temperature to 400 ° F and set the timer to 10 minutes.

5- After 7 minutes, cover with foil if the bread starts to get too dark.

6- Remove and let cool at least 30 minutes. Drizzle with remaining butter and serve.

Nutrition facts per serving

Calories: 292; Fat: 23.4 g; Protein: 13.1 g; Carb: 3.6 g; Fiber: 4 g

Sausage-Stuffed Mushroom Caps

Hands-On Time: **10 minutes**; *Cook Time:* **8 minutes**; *Yield:* **2 servings**.

Ingredients

• 6 large portobello mushroom caps

• ½ pound Italian sausage

• ¼ cup chopped onion

• 2 tablespoons blanched finely ground almond flour

• ¼ cup grated Parmesan cheese

• 1 teaspoon minced fresh garlic

Preparation

1- Use a spoon to dig each mushroom cap while reserving scrapings.

2- In medium skillet over medium heat, brown sausage for about 10 minutes or until cooked through and remaining pink. Drain and add the mushroom pieces, onion, almond flour, Parmesan and garlic reserved. Gently stir in the ingredients and continue cooking for another minute, then remove from heat.

3- Spread the mixture evenly in mushroom caps and place the hats in a 6-inch round pan. Place the pan in the basket of the fryer.

4- Set the temperature to 375 ° F and set the timer to 8 minutes.

5- Once the cooking is over, the trays will be golden and bubbling. Serve hot.

Nutrition facts per serving

Calories: 404

Fat: 25.8 g

Protein: 24.3 g

Carb: 13.7 g

Fiber: 4.5 g

Garlic Herb Butter Roasted Radishes

Hands-On Time: **10 minutes**; *Cook Time:* **10 minutes**; *Yield*: **4 servings**.

Ingredients

- 1 pound radishes

- 2 tablespoons unsalted butter, melted

- ½ teaspoon garlic powder

- ½ teaspoon dried parsley

- ¼ teaspoon dried oregano

- ¼ teaspoon ground black pepper

Preparation

1- Remove the roots from the radishes and cut them into quarters.

2- In a small bowl, add the butter and seasonings. Mix the radishes in the herb butter and place them in the basket of the air fryer.

3- Set the temperature to 350 ° F and set the timer to 10 minutes.

4- Halfway through cooking, mix radishes in the fryer basket. Continue cooking until the edges begin to brown.

5- Serve hot.

Nutrition facts per serving

Calories: 63

Fat: 5.4 g

Protein: 0.7 g

Carb: 1.6 g

Fiber: 1.3 g

CHICKEN MAIN DISHES

Chicken is probably already one of the most consumed meats in your household. It is difficult to compete with its affordability and convenience. In addition, chicken is an excellent source of protein and can also be an excellent source of fat! The problem? The chicken can get a little boring. Fortunately, this chapter is full of healthy and exciting ideas that will bring a new light to dinner. From buffalo chicken crisp chicken fillets to chicken pizza crust, you will not miss out on extraordinary meals to add to your weekly rotation!

Quick Chicken Fajitas

Hands-On Time: **10 minutes**; *Cook Time:* **15 minutes**; *Yield*: **2 servings**.

Ingredients

• 10 ounces boneless, skinless chicken breast, sliced into ¼-in strips

• 2 tablespoons coconut oil, melted

• 1 tablespoon chili powder

• ½ teaspoon cumin

• ½ teaspoon paprika

• ½ teaspoon garlic powder

• ¼ medium onion, peeled and sliced

• ½ green bell pepper, seeded and sliced

• ½ red bell pepper, seeded and sliced

Preparation

1- Place the chicken and coconut oil in a large bowl and sprinkle with chili powder, cumin, paprika and garlic powder. Stir the chicken until it is well seasoned. Place the chicken in the basket of the fryer.

2- Set the temperature to 350 ° F and set the timer to 15 minutes.

3- Add the onion and peppers to the fryer basket when 7 minutes remain on the timer.

4- Mix the chicken two or three times during cooking. Vegetables should be tender and the chicken fully cooked to an internal temperature of at least 165 ° F when finished. Serve hot.

Nutrition facts per serving

Calories: 326

Fat: 15.9 g

Protein: 33.5 g

Carb: 5.2 g

Fiber: 3.2 g

Chicken Patties

Hands-On Time: **15 minutes**; *Cook Time:* **12 minutes***; Yield*: **4 servings**.

Ingredients

- 1 pound ground chicken thigh meat
- ½ cup shredded mozzarella cheese
- 1 teaspoon dried parsley
- ½ teaspoon garlic powder
- ¼ teaspoon onion powder
- 1 large egg
- 2 ounces pork rinds, finely ground

Preparation

1- In a large bowl, combine ground chicken, mozzarella, parsley, garlic powder and onion powder. Form into four patties.

2- Place the patties in the freezer for 15 to 20 minutes until they begin to firm up.

3- Whisk the egg in a medium bowl. Place the chopped pork rinds in a large bowl.

4- Dip each chicken patty in the egg, then squeeze in the pork zest to coat well. Place the patties in the basket of the fryer.

5- Set the temperature to 360 ° F and set the timer to 12 minutes.

6- Patties will be firm and cooked to an internal temperature of 165 ° F when cooked. Serve immediately.

Nutrition facts per serving

Calories: 304

Fat: 17.4 g

Protein: 32.7 g

Carb: 0.8 g

Fiber: 0.1 g

Greek Chicken Stir-Fry

Hands-On Time: **15 minutes**; *Cook Time:* **15 minutes**; *Yield*: **2 servings**.

Ingredients

- 1 (6-ounce) chicken breast, cut into 1-in cubes
- ½ medium zucchini chopped
- ½ red bell pepper, seeded and chopped
- ¼ medium red onion, peeled and sliced
- 1 tablespoon coconut oil
- 1 teaspoon dried oregano
- ½ teaspoon garlic powder
- ¼ teaspoon dried thyme

Preparation

1- Place all the ingredients in a large bowl and mix until the coconut oil covers the meat and vegetables. Pour the contents of the bowl into the basket of the air fryer.

2- Set the temperature to 375 ° F and set the timer to 15 minutes.

3- Shake the fryer basket halfway through the cooking time to distribute the food. Serve immediately.

Nutrition facts per serving

Calories: 186

Fat: 8 g

Protein: 20.4 g

Carb: 3.9 g

Fiber: 1.7 g

Chicken Tenders

Hands-On Time: **8 minutes**; *Cook Time:* **10 minutes**; *Yield*: **2 servings**.

Ingredients

- 1 pound chicken tenders
- 2 eggs
- 1 cup fine almond flour
- 2 tablespoon ground flax seed
- 1 teaspoon Italian seasoning
- 1 teaspoon salt
- 1 teaspoon paprika
- ½ teaspoon ground black pepper
- ½ teaspoon garlic powder
- ½ teaspoon onion powder
- Avocado oil spray

Preparation

1- Blot the chicken with a paper towel and season with a pinch of salt and pepper.

2- In a medium bowl, whisk the eggs.

3- In a large, shallow container, whisk almond flour, flaxseed, and seasoning until mixture is smooth.

4- Dip the chicken into slices in the egg, then spread it in the flour mixture. Repeat until all the chicken is coated.

5- Spray a generous amount of avocado on the basket of the air fryer and place as many chicken fillets in the basket that will fit well with plenty of space. Spray the fillets with an additional avocado spray to lightly coat.

6- Fry for 10 minutes, turning once to 5 minutes.

7- Repeat with the remaining chicken fillets until they have all been cooked to an internal temperature of 165 ° F.

8- Serve with your favorite dip.

Nutrition facts per serving

Calories: 160; Fat: 4.4 g; Protein: 27.3 g; Carb: 0.6 g; Fiber: 0.4 g

Chicken Pizza Crust

Hands-On Time: **10 minutes**; *Cook Time:* **24 minutes**; *Yield*: **4 servings**.

Ingredients

• 1 pound ground chicken thigh meat

• ¼ cup grated Parmesan cheese

• ½ cup shredded mozzarella

Preparation

1- In a large bowl, combine all ingredients. Separate into four equal parts.

2- Cut out four circles of parchment (6 inches) and squeeze each portion of the chicken mixture onto one of the circles. Place them in the basket of the air fryer, working in batches as needed.

3- Set the temperature to 375 ° F and set the timer to 25 minutes.

4- Turn the crust halfway through cooking.

5- Once cooked, you can garnish with cheese and your favorite toppings and cook for another 5 minutes. You can also place the crust in the refrigerator or freezer and cover it at the time of consumption.

Nutrition facts per serving

Calories: 230

Fat: 12.8 g

Protein: 24.7 g

Carb: 1.2 g

Fiber: 0 g

Teriyaki Wings

Hands-On Time: **1 hour**; *Cook Time:* **25 minutes**; *Yield*: **4 servings**.

Ingredients

• 2 pounds chicken wings

• ½ cup sugar-free teriyaki sauce

• 2 teaspoons minced garlic

• ¼ teaspoon ground ginger

• 2 teaspoons baking powder

Preparation

1- Place all ingredients except baking powder in a large bowl or bag and marinate 1 hour in the refrigerator.

2- Place the wings in the deep fryer basket and sprinkle with baking powder. Gently rub in the wings.

3- Set the temperature to 400 ° F and set the timer to 25 minutes.

4- Stir the basket two or three times during cooking.

5- The wings should be crisp and cooked to a minimum internal temperature of 165 ° F at the end of cooking. Serve immediately.

Nutrition facts per serving

Calories: 446

Fat: 29.8 g

Protein: 41.8 g

Carb: 3.1 g

Fiber: 0.1 g

Keto Fried Chicken

Hands-On Time: **10 minutes**; *Cook Time:* **20 minutes***; Yield*: **10 servings**.

Ingredients

- 5 pounds chicken

- 1 cup almond milk

- 1 tablespoon white vinegar

- 2 cups crushed pork rinds

- ½ teaspoon salt

- ½ teaspoon thyme

- ½ teaspoon basil

- ⅓ teaspoon oregano

- 1 teaspoon celery salt

- 1 teaspoon black pepper

- 1 teaspoon dried mustard

- 4 teaspoon paprika

- 2 teaspoon garlic salt

- 1 teaspoon ground ginger

- 3 teaspoons white pepper

- 1 tablespoon coconut oil

Preparation

1- Place the chicken in a large bowl. Mix the almond milk and vinegar and pour over the chicken. Then let the chicken soak in the liquid for 2 hours in the refrigerator.

2- In a shallow bowl or dish, combine pork rinds, salt, thyme, basil, oregano, celery salt, black pepper, dried mustard, paprika, salt garlic, ground ginger and white pepper.

3- Dip each piece of chicken in the dry pork rind mixture until it is well coated.

4- Spread 1 tablespoon of coconut oil in the bottom of the basket of the air fryer.

5- Arrange the chicken in one layer on the basket.

6- Fry in the air at 360 ° F for 10 minutes rotate, then fry in the air for another 10 minutes. Test the chicken temperature to 165 ° F and continue cooking if necessary.

Nutrition facts per serving

Calories: 539

Fat: 11 g

Protein: 45 g

Carb: 1 g

Fiber: 0.1 g

Chicken Enchiladas

Hands-On Time: **20 minutes**; *Cook Time:* **10 minutes**; *Yield*: **4 servings**.

Ingredients

- 1½ cups shredded cooked chicken

- ⅓ cup low-carb enchilada sauce, divided

- ½ pound medium-sliced deli chicken

- 1 cup shredded medium Cheddar cheese

- ½ cup shredded Monterey jack cheese

- ½ cup full-fat sour cream

- 1 medium avocado, peeled, pitted, and sliced

Preparation

1- In a large bowl, combine the shredded chicken and half of the enchilada sauce. Spread spicy chicken slices on a work surface and place 2 tablespoons of the grated chicken mixture on each slice.

2- Sprinkle 2 tablespoons of Cheddar on each roll. Roll gently closed.

3- In a 4-cup baking dish, place each roll, seam down. Pour the remaining sauce over the buns and garnish with Monterey Jack. Place the dish in the basket of the fryer.

4- Set the temperature to 370 ° F and set the timer to 10 minutes.

5- Enchiladas will be golden on top and will boil when cooked. Serve hot with sour cream and avocado slices.

Nutrition facts per serving

Calories: 416; Fat: 25.2 g; Protein: 34.2 g; Carb: 4.2 g; Fiber: 2.3 g

Italian Chicken Thighs

Hands-On Time: **5 minutes**; *Cook Time:* **20 minutes**; *Yield*: **2 servings**.

Ingredients

• 4 bone-in, skin-on chicken thighs

• 2 tablespoons unsalted butter, melted

• 1 teaspoon dried parsley

• 1 teaspoon dried basil

• ½ teaspoon garlic powder

• ¼ teaspoon onion powder

• ¼ teaspoon dried oregano

Preparation

1- Brush chicken legs with butter and sprinkle remaining ingredients over thighs. Place the legs in the basket of the air fryer.

2- Set the temperature to 380 ° F and set the timer to 20 minutes.

3- Halfway through, flip thighs.

4- Once cooked, the internal temperature will be at least 165 ° F and the skin will be crisp. Serve hot.

Nutrition facts per serving

Calories: 596

Fat: 30.9 g

Protein: 68.3 g

Carb: 0.8 g

Fiber: 0.4 g

Pepperoni and Chicken Pizza Bake

Hands-On Time: **10 minutes**; *Cook Time:* **15 minutes**; *Yield*: **4 servings**.

Ingredients

• 2 cups cubed cooked chicken

• 20 slice pepperoni

• 1 cup low-carb, sugar-free pizza sauce

• 1 cup shredded mozzarella cheese

• ¼ cup grated Parmesan cheese

Preparation

1- In a 4-cup baking dish, add the chicken, pepperoni and pizza sauce. Stir so that the meat is completely covered with sauce.

2- Garnish with grated mozzarella and Parmesan cheese. Place the dish in the basket of the fryer.

3- Set the temperature to 375 ° F and set the timer to 15 minutes.

4- The dish will be brown and boiling when cooked. Serve immediately.

Nutrition facts per serving

Calories: 353

Fat: 17.4 g

Protein: 34.4 g

Carb: 6.5 g

Fiber: 1 g

Chicken Parmesan

Hands-On Time: **10 minutes**; *Cook Time:* **24 minutes**; *Yield*: **4 servings**.

Ingredients

• 2 (6-ounce) boneless, skinless chicken breasts

• ½ teaspoon garlic powder

• ¼ teaspoon dried oregano

• ½ teaspoon dried parsley

• 4 tablespoons full-fat mayonnaise divided

• 1 cup shredded mozzarella cheese, divided

• 1 ounce pork rinds crushed

• ½ cup grated Parmesan cheese, divided

• 1 cup low-carb, no-sugar-added pasta sauce

Preparation

1- Cut each chicken breast in half lengthwise and spread out ¾-inch thick. Sprinkle with garlic powder, oregano and parsley.

2- Spread 1 tablespoon mayonnaise on each piece of chicken, then sprinkle ¼ cup of mozzarella on each piece.

3- In a small bowl, combine crushed pork rinds and Parmesan cheese. Sprinkle the mixture over the mozzarella.

4- Pour the sauce into a 6-inch round pan and place the chicken in it. Place the pan in the basket of the fryer.

5- Set the temperature to 320 ° F and set the timer to 25 minutes.

6- The cheese will be browned and the internal temperature of the chicken will be at least 165 ° F at the end of cooking. Serve hot.

Nutrition facts per serving

Calories: 393

Fat: 22.8 g

Protein: 34.2 g

Carb: 4.7 g

Fiber: 2.1 g

Crispy Buffalo Chicken Tenders

Hands-On Time: **15 minutes**; *Cook Time:* **20 minutes**; *Yield*: **4 servings**.

Ingredients

- 1 pound boneless, skinless chicken tenders
- ¼ cup hot sauce
- 1½ ounces pork rinds, finely ground
- 1 teaspoon chili powder
- 1 teaspoon garlic powder

Preparation

1- Place the chicken fillets in a large bowl and pour the hot sauce over them. Mix the fillets with the spicy sauce and coat well.

2- In a large bowl, mix the chopped pork rinds with the chili powder and garlic powder.

3- Place each appendix in chopped pork rinds, covering completely. Wet your hands with water and squeeze the pork rinds into the chicken.

4- Place the bids in a single layer in the fryer basket.

5- Set the temperature to 375 ° F and set the timer to 20 minutes.

6- Serve hot.

Nutrition facts per serving

Calories: 160

Fat: 4.4 g

Protein: 27.3 g

Carb: 0.6 g

Fiber: 0.4 g

Buffalo Chicken Cheese Sticks

Hands-On Time: **5 minutes**; *Cook Time:* **8 minutes**; *Yield*: **2 servings**.

Ingredients

- 1 cup shredded cooked chicken
- ¼ cup buffalo sauce
- 1 cup shredded mozzarella cheese
- 1 large egg
- ¼ cup crumbled feta

Preparation

1- In a large bowl, combine all ingredients except feta cheese. Cut a piece of parchment to fit your air fryer basket and press the mixture into a ½-inch thick circle.

2- Sprinkle the feta mixture and place in the basket of the air fryer.

3- Set the temperature to 400 ° F and set the timer to 8 minutes.

4- After 5 minutes, flip over the cheese mixture.

5- Allow to cool 5 minutes before cutting into sticks. Serve hot.

Nutrition facts per serving

Calories: 369

Fat: 21.5 g

Protein: 35.7 g

Carb: 2.2 g

Fiber: 0 g

Almond-Crusted Chicken

Hands-On Time: **15 minutes**; *Cook Time:* **25 minutes**; *Yield*: **4 servings**.

Ingredients

- ¼ cup slivered almonds

- 2 (6-ounce) boneless, skinless chicken breasts

- 2 tablespoons full-fat mayonnaise

- 1 tablespoon Dijon mustard

Preparation

1- Pulse the almonds in a food processor or chop them until they are finely chopped. Place the almonds evenly on a plate and set aside.

2- Cut each chicken breast in half lengthwise.

3- Mix the mayonnaise and mustard in a small bowl, then wrap the chicken in the mixture.

4- Place each piece of chicken in the chopped almonds to coat them. Gently move the pieces into the fryer basket.

5- Set the temperature to 350 ° F and set the timer to 25 minutes.

6- The chicken will be cooked when it reaches an internal temperature of 165 ° F or higher. Serve hot.

Nutrition facts per serving

Calories: 195

Fat: 10.1 g

Protein: 20.9 g

Carb: 1 g

Fiber: 0.8 g

Blackened Cajun Chicken Tenders

Hands-On Time: **10 minutes**; *Cook Time:* **17 minutes**; *Yield*: **4 servings**.

Ingredients

• 2 teaspoon paprika

• 1 teaspoon chili powder

• ½ teaspoon garlic powder

• ½ teaspoon dried thyme

• ¼ teaspoon onion powder

• ⅛ teaspoon ground cayenne pepper

• 2 tablespoons coconut oil

• 1 pound boneless, skinless chicken tenders

• ¼ cup full-fat ranch dressing

Preparation

1- Pulse the almonds in a food processor or chop them until they are finely chopped. Place the almonds evenly on a plate and set aside.

2- Cut each chicken breast in half lengthwise.

3- Mix the mayonnaise and mustard in a small bowl, then wrap the chicken in the mixture.

4- Place each piece of chicken in the chopped almonds to coat them. Gently move the pieces into the fryer basket.

5- Set the temperature to 350 ° F and set the timer to 25 minutes.

6- The chicken will be cooked when it reaches an internal temperature of 165 ° F or higher. Serve hot.

Nutrition facts per serving

Calories: 163

Fat: 7.5 g

Protein: 21.2 g

Carb: 0.7 g

Fiber: 0.8 g

Lemon Thyme Roasted Chicken

Hands-On Time: **10 minutes**; *Cook Time:* **60 minutes**; *Yield*: **6 servings**.

Ingredients

• 1 (4-pound) chicken

• 2 teaspoons dried thyme

• 1 teaspoon garlic powder

• ½ teaspoon onion powder

• 2 teaspoons dried parsley

• 1 teaspoon baking powder

• 1 medium lemon

• 2 tablespoons salted butter, melted

Preparation

1- Rub the chicken with thyme, garlic powder, onion powder, parsley and baking powder.

2- Slice the lemon and place four slices on the chicken, chest up, and secure with toothpicks. Place the remaining slices inside the chicken.

3- Place the whole chicken in the fryer basket with the breast down.

4- Set the temperature to 350 ° F and set the timer to 60 minutes.

5- After 30 minutes, turn the chicken over so that the side of the breast is in place.

6- Once finished, the internal temperature should be 165 ° F and the skin golden and crisp. To serve, pour the melted butter over the whole chicken.

Nutrition facts per serving

Calories: 504

Fat: 36.8 g

Protein: 32 g

Carb: 1.1 g

Fiber: 0.3 g

Chicken, Spinach, and Feta Bites

Hands-On Time: **10 minutes**; *Cook Time:* **12 minutes**; *Yield*: **4 servings**.

Ingredients

- 1 pound ground chicken thigh meat
- ⅓ cup frozen spinach, thawed and drained
- ⅓ cup crumbled feta
- ¼ teaspoon onion powder
- ½ teaspoon garlic powder
- ½ ounce pork rinds, finely ground

Preparation

1- Mix all ingredients in a large bowl. Roll in 2-inch balls and place in the basket of the air fryer, working in batches if necessary.

2- Set the temperature to 350 ° F and set the timer to 12 minutes.

3- Once completed, the internal temperature will be 165 ° F. Serve immediately.

Nutrition facts per serving

Calories: 220

Fat: 12.2 g

Protein: 24.1 g

Carb: 1.1 g

Fiber: 0.4 g

Cilantro Lime Chicken Thighs

Hands-On Time: **15 minutes**; *Cook Time:* **22 minutes**; *Yield*: **4 servings**.

Ingredients

• 4 bone-in, skin-on chicken thighs

• 1 teaspoon baking powder

• ½ teaspoon garlic powder

• 2 teaspoon chili powder

• 1 teaspoon cumin

• 2 medium limes

• ¼ cup chopped fresh cilantro

Preparation

1- Dry the chicken legs and sprinkle with baking powder.

2- In a small bowl, combine the garlic powder, chili powder and cumin and spread evenly over the legs, rubbing gently over and under the skin of the chicken.

3- Cut a lime in half and squeeze the juice on the thighs. Place the chicken in the basket of the fryer.

4- Set the temperature to 380 ° F and set the timer to 22 minutes.

5- Cut the other lime into quarters to serve and garnish the cooked chicken quarters and coriander.

Nutrition facts per serving

Calories: 435

Fat: 29.1 g

Protein: 32.3 g

Carb: 2 g

Fiber: 0.6 g

Lemon Pepper Drumsticks

Hands-On Time: **5 minutes**; *Cook Time:* **25 minutes**; *Yield*: **8 drumsticks**.

Ingredients

- 2 teaspoons baking powder

- ½ teaspoon garlic powder

- 8 chicken drumsticks

- 4 tablespoons salted butter, melted

- 1 tablespoon lemon pepper seasoning

Preparation

1- Sprinkle baking powder and garlic powder on the drumsticks and rub them against the skin of the chicken. Place the pestles in the basket of the fryer.

2- Set the temperature to 375 ° F and set the timer to 25 minutes.

3- Use tongs to turn the drumsticks halfway through cooking.

4- When the skin is golden and the internal temperature is at least 165 ° F, remove it from the fryer.

5- In a large bowl, mix butter and lemon pepper seasoning. Add the pestles to the bowl and mix until well coated. Serve hot.

Nutrition facts per serving

Calories: 532

Fat: 32.3 g

Protein: 48.3 g

Carb: 1.2 g

Fiber: 0 g

Fajita-Stuffed Chicken Breast

Hands-On Time: **15 minutes**; *Cook Time:* **25 minutes**; *Yield*: **4 servings**.

Ingredients

• 2 (6-ounce) boneless, skinless chicken breasts

• ¼ medium white onion, peeled and sliced

• 1 green bell pepper, seeded and sliced

• 1 tablespoon coconut oil

• 2 teaspoon chili powder

• 1 teaspoon ground cumin

• ½ teaspoon garlic powder

Preparation

1- Cut each chicken breast in half lengthwise. Using a meat tenderizer, pound the chicken until it is about ¼-inch thick.

2- Arrange each slice of chicken on the outside and place three slices of onion and four slices of green pepper at the end closest to you. Start rolling the peppers and onions in the chicken. Secure the roll with toothpicks or a few pieces of butcher's string.

3- Pour coconut oil over the chicken. Sprinkle each side with chili powder, cumin and garlic powder. Place each roll in the basket of the air fryer.

4- Set the temperature to 350 ° F and set the timer to 25 minutes.

5- Serve hot.

Nutrition facts per serving

Calories: 146

Fat: 4.9 g

Protein: 19.8 g

Carb: 2 g

Fiber: 1.2 g

Chicken Cordon Bleu Casserole

Hands-On Time: **15 minutes**; *Cook Time:* **15 minutes**; *Yield*: **4 servings**.

Ingredients

• 2 cups cubed cooked chicken thigh meat

• ½ cup cubed cooked ham

• 2 ounces Swiss cheese, cubed

• 4 ounces full-fat cream cheese, softened

• 1 tablespoon heavy cream

• 2 tablespoons unsalted butter, melted

• 2 teaspoons Dijon mustard

• 1 ounce pork rinds crushed

Preparation

1- Place the chicken and ham in a 6-inch round pan and mix well with the meat and sprinkle with cheese in cubes.

2- In a large bowl, combine the cream cheese, heavy cream, butter and mustard, then pour the mixture over the meat and cheese. Garnish with pork rind. Place the pan in the basket of the fryer.

3- Set the temperature to 350 ° F and set the timer to 15 minutes.

4- The pan will be golden and bubbling when finished. Serve hot.

Nutrition facts per serving

Calories: 403

Fat: 28.2 g

Protein: 30.7 g

Carb: 2.3 g

Fiber: 0 g

Jalapeño Popper Hasselback Chicken

Hands-On Time: **20 minutes**; *Cook Time:* **20 minutes**; *Yield*: **2 servings**.

Ingredients

• 4 slices sugar-free bacon, cooked and crumbled

• 2 ounces full-fat cream cheese, softened

• ½ cup shredded sharp Cheddar cheese, divided

• ¼ cup sliced pickled jalapeños

• 2 (6-ounce) boneless, skinless chicken breasts

Preparation

1- In a medium bowl, put the cooked bacon, then add the cream cheese, half of the cheddar cheese and the slices of jalapeño.

2- Using a sharp knife, slit chicken breasts about ¾ full, being careful not to cut them completely. Depending on the size of the chicken breast, you will probably have 6 to 8 slots per breast.

3- Pour the cream cheese mixture into the chicken slots. Sprinkle the rest of the grated cheese on the chicken breasts and place in the basket of the air fryer.

4- Set the temperature to 350 ° F and set the timer to 20 minutes.

5- Serve hot.

Nutrition facts per serving

Calories: 501

Fat: 25.3 g

Protein: 53.8 g

Carb: 1.4 g

Fiber: 0.2 g

Spinach and Feta-Stuffed Chicken Breast

Hands-On Time: **15 minutes**; *Cook Time:* **25 minutes**; *Yield*: **2 servings**.

Ingredients

- 1 tablespoon unsalted butter

- 5 ounces frozen spinach, thawed and drained

- ½ teaspoon garlic powder divided

- ½ teaspoon salt, divided

- ¼ cup chopped yellow onion

- ¼ cup crumbled feta

- 2 (6-ounce) boneless, skinless chicken breasts

- 1 tablespoon coconut oil

Preparation

1- In a medium skillet over medium heat, add the butter to the pan and fry the spinach for 3 minutes. Sprinkle ¼ teaspoon of garlic powder and ¼ teaspoon of salt over spinach and add the onion to the pan.

2- Continue to sauté for another 3 minutes, then remove from heat and place in a medium bowl. Add the feta cheese to the spinach mixture.

3- Slice a slit about 4 inches lengthwise of each chicken breast. Pour half of the mixture into each piece and tightly close with a couple of toothpicks. Sprinkle the chicken with the rest of the garlic powder and salt. Sprinkle with coconut oil. Place the chicken breasts in the basket of the air fryer.

4- Set the temperature to 350 ° F and set the timer to 25 minutes.

5- When the chicken is fully cooked, it should be golden brown and have an internal temperature of at least 165 ° F. Slice and serve hot.

Nutrition facts per serving

Calories: 393

Fat: 18.5 g

Protein: 43.9 g

Carb: 3.7 g

Fiber: 2.5 g

Southern Fried Chicken

Hands-On Time: **15 minutes**; *Cook Time:* **25 minutes***; Yield*: **4 servings**.

Ingredients

• 2 (6-ounce) boneless, skinless chicken breasts

• 2 tablespoons hot sauce

• 1 tablespoon chili powder

• ½ teaspoon cumin

• ¼ teaspoon onion powder

• ¼ teaspoon ground black pepper

• 2 ounces pork rinds, finely ground

Preparation

1- Cut each chicken breast in half lengthwise. Place the chicken in a large bowl and drizzle with hot sauce.

2- In a small bowl, combine the chili powder, cumin, onion powder and pepper. Sprinkle over the chicken.

3- Place the chopped pork rinds in a large bowl and dip each piece of chicken into the bowl, wrapping as much as possible. Place the chicken in the basket of the fryer.

4- Set the temperature to 350 ° F and set the timer to 25 minutes.

5- Halfway through cooking, turn chicken over carefully.

6- When finished, the internal temperature will be at least 165 ° F and the coating of the pork rind will be dark golden brown. Serve hot.

Nutrition facts per serving

Calories: 192

Fat: 6.9 g

Protein: 27.8 g

Carb: 0.7 g

Fiber: 0.9 g

BEEF AND PORK MAIN DISHES

Beef and pork are two meats already brimming with flavors that you can still improve with your air fryer. Who would have thought that it would be possible to get tender and juicy pork chops in a few minutes? These versatile meats can be used to create classics in the blink of an eye, as well as exciting new dishes that are high in protein and fat. With recipes ranging from Bacon Cheeseburger Casserole to easy and juicy pork chops, this chapter will help you strengthen your culinary repertoire in no time!

Pub-Style Burger

Hands-On Time: **10 minutes**; *Cook Time:* **10 minutes**; *Yield*: **4 servings**.

Ingredients

- 1 pound ground sirloin
- ½ teaspoon salt
- ¼ teaspoon ground black pepper
- 2 tablespoons salted butter, melted
- ½ cup full-fat mayonnaise
- 2 teaspoons sriracha
- ¼ teaspoon garlic powder
- 8 large leaves butter lettuce
- 4 Bacon-Wrapped Onion Rings
- 8 slices pickle

Preparation

1- In a medium bowl, combine the sirloin, salt and pepper. Form four patties. Brush with butter and place in the deep fryer basket.

2- Set the temperature to 380 ° F and set the timer to 10 minutes.

3- Turn the patties to half the cooking time for an average hamburger. Add another 3 to 5 minutes to do well.

4- In a small bowl, combine mayonnaise, sriracha and garlic powder. Put aside.

5- Place each cooked burger on a lettuce leaf and cover with onion rings, two gherkins and a spoonful of your prepared burger sauce. Wrap another lettuce leaf firmly to hold. Serve hot.

Nutrition facts per serving

Calories: 442

Fat: 34.9 g

Protein: 22.3 g

Carb: 3.3 g

Fiber: 0.8 g

Pigs in a Blanket

Hands-On Time: **10 minutes**; *Cook Time:* **7 minutes**; *Yield*: **2 servings**.

Ingredients

• ½ cup shredded mozzarella cheese

• 2 tablespoons blanched finely ground almond flour

• 1 ounce full-fat cream cheese

• 2 (2-ounce) beef smoked sausages

• ½ teaspoon sesame seeds

Preparation

1- Place the mozzarella, almond flour and cream cheese in a large microwaveable bowl. Microwave for 45 seconds and stir until smooth; Roll the dough into a ball and cut in half.

2- Press each half into a 4 × 5-inch rectangle. Roll one sausage in each half of the dough and press on the closed seams. Sprinkle the top with sesame seeds.

3- Place each packaged sausage in the basket of the air fryer.

4- Set the temperature to 400 ° F and set the timer to 7 minutes.

5- The outside will be golden when fully cooked. Serve immediately.

Nutrition facts per serving

Calories: 405

Fat: 32.2 g

Protein: 17.5 g

Carb: 2.1 g

Fiber: 0.8 g

Crispy Beef and Broccoli Stir-Fry

Hands-On Time: **1 hour**; *Cook Time:* **20 minutes**; *Yield*: **2 servings**.

Ingredients

- ½ pound sirloin steak, thinly sliced

- 2 tablespoons soy sauce

- ¼ teaspoon grated ginger

- ¼ teaspoon finely minced garlic

- 1 tablespoon coconut oil

- 2 cups broccoli florets

- ¼ teaspoon crushed red pepper

- ⅛ teaspoon xanthan gum

- ½ teaspoon sesame seeds

Preparation

1- To marinate the beef, place it in a large bowl or storage bag and add the soy sauce, ginger, garlic and coconut oil. Marinate 1 hour in the refrigerator.

2- Remove the beef from the marinade by reserving the marinade and place the beef in the basket of the air fryer.

3- Set the temperature to 320 ° F and set the timer to 20 minutes.

4- After 10 minutes, add the broccoli and sprinkle red pepper in the deep fryer basket and shake.

5- Pour the marinade into a skillet over medium heat and bring to a boil, then simmer. Stir in xanthan gum and allow to thicken.

6- When the fryer timer sounds, quickly empty the fryer basket into the pan and mix. Sprinkle with sesame seeds. Serve immediately.

Nutrition facts per serving

Calories: 342

Fat: 18.9 g

Protein: 27 g

Carb: 6.9 g

Fiber: 2.7 g

Reverse Seared Ribeye

Hands-On Time: **5 minutes**; *Cook Time:* **45 minutes**; *Yield*: **2 servings**.

Ingredients

- 1 (8-ounce) ribeye steak
- ½ teaspoon pink Himalayan salt
- ¼ teaspoon ground peppercorn
- 1 tablespoon coconut oil
- 1 tablespoon salted butter, softened
- ¼ teaspoon garlic powder
- ½ teaspoon dried parsley
- ¼ teaspoon dried oregano

Preparation

1- Rub the steak with salt and ground pepper. Place in the basket of the air fryer.

2- Set the temperature to 250 ° F and set the timer to 45 minutes.

3- After the timer sounds a beep, first check the cooking and add a few minutes until the internal temperature is your preference.

4- In a medium skillet over medium heat, add coconut oil. When the oil is hot, quickly grasp the outside and sides of the steak until crisp and golden. Remove from heat and let steak rest.

5- In a small bowl, beat the butter with the garlic powder, parsley and oregano.

6- Slice the steak and serve with the herb butter on top.

Nutrition facts per serving

Calories: 377

Fat: 30.7 g

Protein: 22.6 g

Carb: 0.4 g

Fiber: 0.2 g

Empanadas

Hands-On Time: **15 minutes**; *Cook Time:* **10 minutes**; *Yield*: **2 empanadas**.

Ingredients

- 1 pound ground beef
- ¼ cup water
- ¼ cup diced onion
- 2 teaspoon chili powder
- ½ teaspoon garlic powder
- ¼ teaspoon cumin
- 1½ cups shredded mozzarella cheese
- ½ cup blanched finely ground almond flour
- 2 ounces full-fat cream cheese
- 1 large egg

Preparation

1- In a medium skillet over medium heat, brown the ground beef for about 7 to 10 minutes. Drain the fat. Put the pan back on the stove.

2- Add water and onion to the pan. Stir in and sprinkle with chili powder, garlic and cumin. Reduce the heat and simmer for another 3 to 5 minutes; Remove from heat and set aside.

3- In a large microwave-safe bowl, add mozzarella, almond flour and cream cheese. Microwave for 1 minute. Stir until smooth. Form the mixture into a ball.

4- Place the dough between two sheets of parchment paper and spread out ¼-inch thick. Cut the dough into four squares. Place ¼ chopped beef on the bottom half of each square. Fold the dough and roll the edges or press with a wet fork to close.

5- Break the egg into a small bowl and whisk. Brush the egg over the empanadas.

6- Cut out a piece of parchment suitable for your deep fryer basket and place the empanadas on the parchment. Place in the basket of the air fryer.

7- Set the temperature to 400 ° F and set the timer to 10 minutes.

8- Return the empanadas halfway through cooking. Serve hot.

Nutrition facts per serving

Calories: 463; Fat: 30.8 g; Protein: 33.3 g; Carb: 4.3 g; Fiber: 2.2 g

Easy Juicy Pork Chops

Hands-On Time: **5 minutes**; *Cook Time:* **15 minutes**; *Yield*: **2 servings**.

Ingredients

• 1 teaspoon chili powder

• ½ teaspoon garlic powder

• ½ teaspoon cumin

• ¼ teaspoon ground black pepper

• ¼ teaspoon dried oregano

• 2 (4-ounce) boneless pork chops

• 2 tablespoons unsalted butter, divided

Preparation

1- In a small bowl, combine the chili powder, garlic powder, cumin, pepper and oregano. Rub dry on pork chops. Place the pork chops in the deep fryer basket.

2- Set the temperature to 400 ° F and set the timer to 15 minutes.

3- The internal temperature should be at least 145 ° F when fully cooked. Serve warm and garnish with a tablespoon of butter.

Nutrition facts per serving

Calories: 313

Fat: 22.6 g

Protein: 24.4 g

Carb: 1.1 g

Fiber: 0.7 g

Bacon-Wrapped Hot Dog

Hands-On Time: **5 minutes**; *Cook Time:* **10 minutes**; *Yield*: **4 servings**.

Ingredients

• 4 beef hot dogs

• 4 slices sugar-free bacon

Preparation

1- Wrap each hot dog with a slice of bacon and secure with a toothpick. Place in the basket of the air fryer.

2- Set the temperature to 370 ° F and set the timer to 10 minutes.

3- Turn each hot dog halfway through cooking. Once cooked, the bacon will be crisp. Serve hot.

Nutrition facts per serving

Calories: 197

Fat: 15 g

Protein: 9.2 g

Carb: 1.3 g

Fiber: 0 g

Baby Back Ribs

Hands-On Time: **5 minutes**; *Cook Time:* **25 minutes**; *Yield*: **4 servings**.

Ingredients

• 2 pounds baby back ribs

• 2 teaspoon chili powder

• 1 teaspoon paprika

• ½teaspoon onion powder

• ½ teaspoon garlic powder

• ¼ teaspoon ground cayenne pepper

• ½ cup low-carb, sugar-free barbecue sauce

Preparation

1- Rub the ribs with all the ingredients except the barbecue sauce. Place in the basket of the air fryer.

2- Set the temperature to 400 ° F and set the timer to 25 minutes.

3- Once the operation is complete, the ribs are dark and charred at an internal temperature of at least 190 ° F. Brush the ribs with barbecue sauce and serve hot.

Nutrition facts per serving

Calories: 650

Fat: 51.5 g

Protein: 40.1 g

Carb: 2.3 g

Fiber: 0.8 g

Oversized BBQ Meatballs

Hands-On Time: **10 minutes**; *Cook Time:* **14 minutes**; *Yield*: **4 servings**.

Ingredients

- 1 pound ground beef

- ¼ pound ground Italian sausage

- 1 large egg

- ¼ teaspoon onion powder

- ½ teaspoon garlic powder

- 1 teaspoon dried parsley

- 4 slices sugar-free bacon, cooked and chopped

- ¼ cup chopped white onion

- ¼ cup chopped pickled jalapeños

- ½ cup low-carb, sugar-free barbecue sauce

Preparation

1- In a large bowl, combine ground beef, sausages and eggs until combined. Mix all other ingredients except barbecue sauce. Form eight meatballs. Place the meatballs in the basket of the air fryer.

2- Set the temperature to 400 ° F and set the timer to 14 minutes.

3- Turn the meatballs halfway through cooking.

4- Once finished, the meatballs must be browned on the outside and have an internal temperature of at least 180 ° F.

5- Remove the meatballs from the fryer and mix with the barbecue sauce. Serve hot.

Nutrition facts per serving

Calories: 336

Fat: 19.5 g

Protein: 28.1 g

Carb: 4 g

Fiber: 0.4 g

Crispy Pork Chop Salad

Hands-On Time: **15 minutes**; *Cook Time:* **8 minutes**; *Yield*: **2 servings**.

Ingredients

• 1 tablespoon coconut oil

• 2 (4-ounce) pork chops chopped into 1-inch cubes

• 2 teaspoon chili powder

• 1 teaspoon paprika

• ½ teaspoon garlic powder

• ¼ teaspoon onion powder

• 4 cups chopped romaine

• 1 medium Roma tomato, diced

• ½ cup shredded Monterey jack cheese

• 1 medium avocado, peeled, pitted, and diced

• ¼ cup full-fat ranch dressing

• 1 tablespoon chopped cilantro

Preparation

1- In a large bowl, pour the coconut oil over the pork. Sprinkle with chili powder, paprika, garlic powder and onion. Place the pork in the basket of the fryer.

2- Set the temperature to 400 ° F and set the timer to 8 minutes.

3- The pork will be golden and crisp at the end of cooking.

4- In a large bowl, place the slices of romaine, tomato and crispy pork. Garnish with grated cheese and avocado. Pour the ranch vinaigrette around the bowl and mix the salad to coat well.

5- Garnish with coriander. Serve immediately.

Nutrition facts per serving

Calories: 526; Fat: 37 g; Protein: 34.4 g; Carb: 5.2 g; Fiber: 8.6 g

Ground Beef Taco Rolls

Hands-On Time: **20 minutes**; *Cook Time:* **10 minutes**; *Yield*: **4 servings**.

Ingredients

- ½ pound ground beef
- ⅓ cup water
- 1 tablespoon chili powder
- 2 teaspoons cumin
- ½ teaspoon garlic powder
- ¼ teaspoon dried oregano
- ¼ cup canned diced tomatoes and chiles, drained
- 2 tablespoons chopped cilantro
- 1½ cups shredded mozzarella cheese
- ½ cup blanched finely ground almond flour
- 2 ounces full-fat cream cheese
- 1 large egg

Preparation

1- In a medium skillet over medium heat, brown the ground beef for about 7 to 10 minutes. When the meat is completely cooked, drain it.

2- Add water to the pan and add the chili powder, cumin, garlic powder, oregano and tomatoes with the peppers. Add the coriander; Bring to a boil, reduce heat and simmer for 3 minutes.

3- In a large microwave-safe bowl, strain mozzarella, almond flour, cream cheese and eggs. Microwave for 1 minute. Stir the mixture quickly until the dough ball is forming well.

4- Cut a piece of parchment for your work surface. Press the dough into a large rectangle on the parchment, wetting your hands to prevent the dough from sticking as needed. Cut the dough into eight rectangles.

5- On each rectangle, place a few spoons of the meat mixture. Fold the short ends of each roll towards the center and unroll the length like a burrito.

6- Cut out a piece of parchment to fit your air fryer basket. Place the taco rolls on the parchment and place them in the basket of the air fryer.

7- Set the temperature to 360 ° F and set the timer to 10 minutes.

8- Return to mid-cooking.

9- Let cool 10 minutes before serving.

Nutrition facts per serving

Calories: 380

Fat: 26.5 g

Protein: 24.8 g

Carb: 4.5 g

Fiber: 2.5 g

Fajita Flank Steak Rolls

Hands-On Time: **20 minutes**; *Cook Time:* **15 minutes**; *Yield*: **6 servings**.

Ingredients

• 2 pounds flank steak

• 2 tablespoons unsalted butter

• ¼ cup diced yellow onion

• 1 red bell pepper, seeded and sliced

• 1 green bell pepper, seeded and sliced

• 2 teaspoon chili powder

• 1 teaspoon cumin

• ½ teaspoon garlic powder

• 4 (1-ounce) slices pepper jack cheese

Preparation

1- In a medium skillet over medium heat, melt the butter and start browning the onion, red pepper and green pepper. Sprinkle with chili powder, cumin and garlic powder. Sauté until the peppers are tender, about 5 to 7 minutes.

2- Lay flank steak flat on a work surface. Spread the onion and pepper mixture over the entire steak rectangle. Place slices of cheese on onions and peppers, overlapping slightly.

3- Starting at the short end, start rolling the steak by folding the cheese into the roll as needed. Secure the roll with twelve toothpicks, six on each side of the steak roll. Place the roll of steak in the basket of the fryer.

4- Set the temperature to 400 ° F and set the timer to 15 minutes.

5- Rotate the roll halfway through cooking. Add another 1 to 4 minutes depending on your preferred internal temperature (135 ° F for the medium).

6- When the timer rings, let the roller sit for 15 minutes, then cut it into six equal pieces. Serve hot.

Nutrition facts per serving

Calories: 439; Fat: 26.6 g; Protein: 38 g; Carb: 2.5 g; Fiber: 1.2 g

Pulled Pork

Hands-On Time: **10 minutes**; *Cook Time:* **2½ hours**; *Yield:* **8 servings**.

Ingredients

• 2 tablespoons chili powder

• 1 teaspoon garlic powder

• ½ teaspoon onion powder

• ½ teaspoon ground black pepper

• ½ teaspoon cumin

• 1 (4-pound) pork shoulder

Preparation

1- In a small bowl, combine the chili powder, garlic powder, onion powder, pepper and cumin. Rub the spice mixture over the pork shoulder, patting it in the skin. Place the pork shoulder in the basket of the fryer.

2- Set the temperature to 350 ° F and set the timer to 150 minutes.

3- The skin of the pork will be crisp and the meat easily shredded with two forks once cooked. The internal temperature must be at least 145 ° F.

Nutrition facts per serving

Calories: 537

Fat: 35.5 g

Protein: 42.6 g

Carb: 0.7 g

Fiber: 0.8 g

Classic Mini Meatloaf

Hands-On Time: **10 minutes**; *Cook Time:* **25 minutes**; *Yield*: **6 servings**.

Ingredients

• 1 pound ground beef

• ¼ medium yellow onion, peeled and diced

• ½ green bell pepper, seeded and diced

• 1 large egg

• 3 tablespoons blanched finely ground almond flour

• 1 tablespoon Worcestershire sauce

• ½ teaspoon garlic powder

• 1 teaspoon dried parsley

• 2 tablespoons tomato paste

• ¼ cup water

• 1 tablespoon powdered erythritol

Preparation

1- In a large bowl, combine ground beef, onion, pepper, egg and almond flour. Pour the Worcestershire sauce and add the garlic powder and parsley to the bowl. Mix until completely combined.

2- Divide the mixture in half and place in two baking pans.

3- In a small bowl, combine the tomato paste, water and erythritol. Place half of the mixture on each loaf.

4- If necessary, work in batches and place the bread dies in the basket of the air fryer.

5- Set the temperature to 350 ° F and set the timer to 25 minutes or until the internal temperature reaches 180 ° F.

6- Serve hot.

Nutrition facts per serving

Calories: 170; Fat: 9.4 g; Protein: 14.9 g; Carb: 2.6 g; Fiber: 0.9 g

Easy Lasagna Casserole

Hands-On Time: **15 minutes**; *Cook Time:* **15 minutes**; *Yield*: **4 servings**.

Ingredients

- ¾ cup low-carb no-sugar-added pasta sauce

- 1 pound ground beef cooked and drained

- ½ cup full-fat ricotta cheese

- ¼ cup grated Parmesan cheese

- ½ teaspoon garlic powder

- 1 teaspoon dried parsley

- ½ teaspoon dried oregano

- 1 cup shredded mozzarella cheese

Preparation

1- In a 4-cup baking dish, pour ¼ cup of pasta sauce into the bottom of the dish. Place ¼ of the ground beef on the sauce.

2- In a small bowl, combine ricotta, Parmesan cheese, garlic powder, parsley and oregano. Place spoonfuls of half the mixture on the beef.

3- Sprinkle with ⅓ of the mozzarella. Repeat until all beef, ricotta mixture, sauce and mozzarella are used, ending with mozzarella.

4- Cover the dish with aluminum foil and place it in the fryer basket.

5- Set the temperature to 370 ° F and set the timer to 15 minutes.

6- During the last 2 minutes of cooking, remove the foil to brown the cheese. Serve immediately.

Nutrition facts per serving

Calories: 371

Fat: 21.4 g

Protein: 31.4 g

Carb: 4.2 g

Fiber: 1.6 g

Chorizo and Beef Burger

Hands-On Time: **10 minutes**; *Cook Time:* **15 minutes**; *Yield*: **4 servings**.

Ingredients

- ¾ pound ground beef

- ¼ pound Mexican-style ground chorizo

- ¼ cup chopped onion

- 5 slices pickled jalapeños, chopped

- 2 teaspoon chili powder

- 1 teaspoon minced garlic

- ¼ teaspoon cumin

Preparation

1- In a large bowl, combine all ingredients. Divide the mixture into four sections and form into burger patties.

2- Place the burger patties in the fryer basket, working in batches if necessary.

3- Set the temperature to 375 ° F and set the timer to 15 minutes.

4- Turn the patties halfway through cooking. Serve hot.

Nutrition facts per serving

Calories: 291

Fat: 18.3 g

Protein: 21.6 g

Carb: 3.8 g

Fiber: 0.9 g

Crispy Brats

Hands-On Time: **6 minutes**; *Cook Time:* **15 minutes**; *Yield*: **4 servings**.

Ingredients

• 4 (3-ounce) beef bratwursts

Preparation

1- Place the children in the basket of the fryer.

2- Set the temperature to 375 ° F and set the timer to 15 minutes.

3- Serve hot.

Nutrition facts per serving

Calories: 286

Fat: 24.8 g

Protein: 11.8 g

Carb: 0 g

Fiber: 0 g

Breaded Pork Chops

Hands-On Time: **10 minutes**; *Cook Time:* **15 minutes**; *Yield:* **4 servings**.

Ingredients

- 1½ ounces pork rinds, finely ground
- 1 teaspoon chili powder
- ½ teaspoon garlic powder
- 1 tablespoon coconut oil, melted
- 4 (4-ounce) pork chops

Preparation

1- In a large bowl, combine the chopped pork rinds, chili powder and garlic powder.

2- Brush each pork chop with coconut oil, then squeeze into the pork rind mixture by coating both sides. Place each pork chop wrapped in the basket of the air fryer.

3- Set the temperature to 400 ° F and set the timer to 15 minutes.

4- Turn each pork chop halfway through cooking.

5- Once cooked, the pork chops will be browned on the outside and have an internal temperature of at least 145 ° F.

Nutrition facts per serving

Calories: 292

Fat: 18.5 g

Protein: 29.5 g

Carb: 0.3 g

Fiber: 0.3 g

Peppercorn-Crusted Beef Tenderloin

Hands-On Time: **10 minutes**; *Cook Time:* **25 minutes**; *Yield*: **6 servings**.

Ingredients

• 1 (2-pound) beef tenderloin, trimmed of visible fat

• 2 tablespoons salted butter, melted

• 2 teaspoons minced roasted garlic

• 3 tablespoons ground 4-peppercorn blend

Preparation

1- In a small bowl, combine the butter and roasted garlic. Brush the beef tenderloin.

2- Place the ground peppercorns on a plate and roll them into the net to create a crust. Place the tenderloin in the basket of the fryer.

3- Set the temperature to 400 ° F and set the timer to 25 minutes.

4- Turn the tenderloin halfway through cooking.

5- Allow the meat to rest 10 minutes before slicing.

Nutrition facts per serving

Calories: 289

Fat: 13.8 g

Protein: 34.7 g

Carb: 1.6 g

Fiber: 0.9 g

Taco-Stuffed Peppers

Hands-On Time: **15 minutes**; *Cook Time:* **15 minutes**; *Yield*: **4 servings**.

Ingredients

- 1 pound ground beef

- 1 tablespoon chili powder

- 2 teaspoons cumin

- 1 teaspoon garlic powder

- 1 teaspoon salt

- ¼ teaspoon ground black pepper

- 1 can diced tomatoes and green chiles

- 4 green bell peppers

- 1 cup shredded Monterey jack cheese, divided

Preparation

1- In a medium skillet over medium heat, brown the ground beef for about 7 to 10 minutes. When there is no more pink, drain the fat from the pan.

2- Put the pan back on the stove and add the chili powder, cumin, garlic powder, salt and black pepper. Add a box of diced tomatoes and drained peppers to the pan. Continue cooking for 3 to 5 minutes.

3- While the mixture is cooking, cut each pepper in half. Remove the seeds and the white membrane. Pour the cooked mixture evenly into each pepper and garnish with ¼ cup of cheese. Place the stuffed peppers in the basket of the air fryer.

4- Set the temperature to 350 ° F and set the timer to 15 minutes.

5- Once finished, the peppers will be tender and the cheese browned and bubbling. Serve hot.

Nutrition facts per serving

Calories: 346

Fat: 19.1 g

Protein: 27.8 g

Carb: 7.2 g

Fiber: 3.5 g

Italian Stuffed Bell Peppers

Hands-On Time: **15 minutes**; *Cook Time:* **15 minutes**; *Yield*: **4 servings**.

Ingredients

• 1 pound ground pork Italian sausage

• ½ teaspoon garlic powder

• ½ teaspoon dried parsley

• 1 medium Roma tomato, diced

• ¼ cup chopped onion

• 4 green bell peppers

• 1 cup shredded mozzarella cheese, divided

Preparation

1- In medium skillet over medium heat, brown sausage powder about 7 to 10 minutes or until no more pink. Drain the fat from the pan.

2- Put the pan back on the stove and add the garlic powder, parsley, tomatoes and onion. Continue cooking for 3 to 5 minutes.

3- Cut the peppers in half and remove the seeds and the white membrane.

4- Remove the meat mixture from the range and pour it evenly into the pepper halves. Garnish with mozzarella. Place the pepper halves in the basket of the air fryer.

5- Set the temperature to 350 ° F and set the timer to 15 minutes.

6- Once cooked, the peppers will be tender and the cheese golden. Serve hot.

Nutrition facts per serving

Calories: 358

Fat: 24.1 g

Protein: 21.1 g

Carb: 8.7 g

Fiber: 2.6 g

Bacon Cheeseburger Casserole

Hands-On Time: **15 minutes**; *Cook Time:* **20 minutes**; *Yield*: **4 servings**.

Ingredients

- 1 pound ground beef
- ¼ medium white onion, peeled and chopped
- 1 cup shredded Cheddar cheese, divided
- 1 large egg
- 4 slices sugar-free bacon, cooked and crumbled
- 2 pickle spears chopped

Preparation

1- Brown the ground beef in a medium skillet over medium heat for 7 to 10 minutes. When there is no more pink, drain the fat. Remove from heat and add the ground beef in a large mixing bowl.

2- Add the onion, ½-cup cheddar and the egg in a bowl. Mix the ingredients well and add crumbled bacon.

3- Pour the mixture into a round 4-cup baking dish and cover with remaining cheddar cheese. Place in the basket of the air fryer.

4- Set the temperature to 375 ° F and set the timer to 20 minutes.

5- The casserole will be golden on the top and close in the middle once cooked. Serve immediately with the chopped gherkins.

Nutrition facts per serving

Calories: 369

Fat: 22.6 g

Protein: 31 g

Carb: 1 g

Fiber: 0.2 g

FISH AND SEAFOOD MAIN DISHES

Get ready to dive into a sea of delicious recipes! Fish is one of the best sources of omega-3 fatty acids, which can help fight inflammation and heart disease. It is also an excellent source of protein to help you keep your muscles strong during a keto diet. Nevertheless, despite the benefits in terms of taste and health, seafood is not the easiest food to prepare.

Enter the air fryer. The air fryer will be your favorite tool for creating crispy and delicious fish and seafood recipes. From fried tuna salad to firecracker shrimp, you'll soon be a master of seafood cooking creating tasty dishes that your family will never have enough!

Shrimp Scampi

Hands-On Time: **10 minutes**; *Cook Time:* **8 minutes**; *Yield*: **4 servings**.

Ingredients

• 4 tablespoons salted butter

• ½ medium lemon

• 1 teaspoon minced roasted garlic

• ¼ cup heavy whipping cream

• ¼ teaspoon xanthan gum

• ¼ teaspoon red pepper flakes

• 1 pound medium peeled and deveined shrimp

• 1 tablespoon chopped fresh parsley

Preparation

1- In a medium saucepan over medium heat, melt the butter; Zest the lemon, then squeeze the juice into the pan. Add the garlic.

2- Pour the cream, xanthan gum and red pepper flakes; Whisk until the mixture starts to thicken, about 2–3 minutes.

3- Place the shrimp in a round baking dish of 4 cups. Pour the cream sauce over the shrimp and cover with foil. Place the dish in the basket of the air fryer.

4- Set the temperature to 400 ° F and set the timer to 8 minutes.

5- Stir twice during cooking.

6- Once cooked, garnish with parsley and serve hot.

Nutrition facts per serving

Calories: 240

Fat: 17 g

Protein: 16.7 g

Carb: 2 g

Fiber: 0.4 g

Shrimp Kebabs

Hands-On Time: **10 minutes**; *Cook Time:* **7 minutes**; *Yield:* **2 servings**.

Ingredients

• 18 medium shelled and deveined shrimp

• 1 medium zucchini, cut into 1-inch cubes

• ½ red bell pepper, cut into 1-inch-thick squares

• ¼ medium red onion, cut into 1-inch-thick squares

• 1½ tablespoons coconut oil, melted

• 2 teaspoon chili powder

• ½ teaspoon paprika

• ¼ teaspoon ground black pepper

Preparation

1- Soak four 6-inch bamboo skewers in water for 30 minutes; Place a shrimp on the skewer, then a zucchini, a pepper and an onion. Repeat until all ingredients are used.

2- Brush each skewer with coconut oil. Sprinkle with chili powder, paprika and black pepper. Place the skewers in the basket of the air fryer.

3- Set the temperature to 400 ° F and set the timer for 7 minutes or until the shrimp is fully cooked and the vegetables are tender.

4- Turn the skewers halfway through cooking. Serve hot.

Nutrition facts per serving

Calories: 166

Fat: 10.7 g

Protein: 9.5 g

Carb: 5.4 g

Fiber: 3.1 g

Crab Legs

Hands-On Time: **6 minutes**; *Cook Time:* **15 minutes**; *Yield*: **4 servings**.

Ingredients

• ¼ cup salted butter, melted and divided

• 3 pounds crab legs

• ¼ teaspoon garlic powder

• Juice of ½ medium lemon

Preparation

1- In a large bowl, pour 2 tablespoons butter on the crab legs. Place the crab legs in the basket of the fryer.

2- Set the temperature to 400 ° F and set the timer to 15 minutes.

3- Shake the fryer basket to mix the crab legs halfway through cooking.

4- In a small bowl, mix remaining butter, garlic powder and lemon juice.

5- To serve, break the crab legs and remove the meat. Dip in the lemon butter.

Nutrition facts per serving

Calories: 123

Fat: 5.6 g

Protein: 15.7 g

Carb: 0.4 g

Fiber: 0 g

Crab Cakes

Hands-On Time: **10 minutes**; *Cook Time:* **10 minutes**; *Yield*: **4 servings**.

Ingredients

- 2 (6-ounce) cans lump crabmeat

- ¼ cup blanched finely ground almond flour

- 1 large egg

- 2 tablespoons full-fat mayonnaise

- ½ teaspoon Dijon mustard

- ½ tablespoon lemon juice

- ½ green bell pepper, seeded and chopped

- ¼ cup chopped green onion

- ½ teaspoon Old Bay seasoning

Preparation

1- In a large bowl, combine all ingredients. Form four balls and flatten them. Place the patties in the basket of the fryer.

2- Set the temperature to 350 ° F and set the timer to 10 minutes.

3- Turn the patties halfway through cooking. Serve hot.

Nutrition facts per serving

Calories: 151

Fat: 10 g

Protein: 13.4 g

Carb: 1.4 g

Fiber: 0.9 g

Hot Crab Dip

Hands-On Time: **10 minutes**; *Cook Time:* **8 minutes**; *Yield*: **4 servings**.

Ingredients

• 8 ounces full-fat cream cheese, softened

• ¼ cup full-fat mayonnaise

• ¼ cup full-fat sour cream

• 1 tablespoon lemon juice

• ½ teaspoon hot sauce

• ¼ cup chopped pickled jalapeños

• ¼ cup sliced green onion

• 2 (6-ounce) cans lump crabmeat

• ½ cup shredded Cheddar cheese

Preparation

1- Place all ingredients in a 4 cup round baking dish and stir until everything is well mixed. Place the dish in the basket of the fryer.

2- Set the temperature to 400 ° F and set the timer to 8 minutes.

3- Dip will be bubbling and hot when finished. Serve hot.

Nutrition facts per serving

Calories: 441

Fat: 33.8 g

Protein: 17.8 g

Carb: 7.6 g

Fiber: 0.6 g

Almond Pesto Salmon

Hands-On Time: **5 minutes**; *Cook Time:* **12 minutes**; *Yield*: **2 servings**.

Ingredients

• ¼ cup pesto

• ¼ cup sliced almonds, roughly chopped

• 2 salmon fillets (about 4 ounces each)

• 2 tablespoons unsalted butter, melted

Preparation

1- In a small bowl, mix pesto and almonds. Put aside.

2- Place the fillets in a 6-inch round baking dish.

3- Brush each fillet with butter and place half of the pesto mixture on each fillet. Place the dish in the basket of the fryer.

4- Set the temperature to 390 ° F and set the timer to 12 minutes.

5- The salmon will come off easily once cooked and will reach an internal temperature of at least 145 ° F. Serve hot.

Nutrition facts per serving

Calories: 433

Fat: 34 g

Protein: 23.3 g

Carb: 3.7 g

Fiber: 2.4 g

Spicy Salmon Jerky

Hands-On Time: **5 minutes**; *Cook Time:* **4 hours**; *Yield*: **4 servings**.

Ingredients

• 1 pound salmon, skin and bones removed

• ¼ cup soy sauce

• ½ teaspoon liquid smoke

• ¼ teaspoon ground black pepper

• Juice of ½ medium lime

• ½ teaspoon ground ginger

• ¼ teaspoon red pepper flakes

Preparation

1- Cut the salmon into ¼-inch-thick slices, 4 inches long.

2- Place the strips in a large storage bag or covered bowl and add the remaining ingredients. Marinate for 2 hours in the refrigerator.

3- Place each strip in the basket of the air fryer in a single layer.

4- Set the temperature to 140 ° F and set the timer to 4 hours.

5- Cool and store in a sealed container until ready to eat.

Nutrition facts per serving

Calories: 108

Fat: 4.1 g

Protein: 15.1 g

Carb: 0.8 g

Fiber: 0.2 g

Salmon Patties

Hands-On Time: **10 minutes**; *Cook Time:* **8 minutes**; *Yield*: **2 servings**.

Ingredients

• 2 (5-ounce) pouches cooked pink salmon

• 1 large egg

• ¼ cup ground pork rinds

• 2 tablespoons full-fat mayonnaise

• 2 teaspoons sriracha

• 1 teaspoon chili powder

Preparation

1- Combine all ingredients in a large bowl and form four patties. Place the patties in the basket of the fryer.

2- Set the temperature to 400 ° F and set the timer to 8 minutes.

3- Carefully turn each cake halfway through cooking. The patties will be crispy on the outside once cooked.

Nutrition facts per serving

Calories: 319

Fat: 19 g

Protein: 33.8 g

Carb: 1.4 g

Fiber: 0.5 g

Cajun Salmon

Hands-On Time: **5 minutes**; *Cook Time:* **7 minutes**; *Yield:* **2 servings**.

Ingredients

• 2 (4-ounce) salmon fillets, skin removed

• 2 tablespoons unsalted butter, melted

• ⅛ teaspoon ground cayenne pepper

• ½ teaspoon garlic powder

• 1 teaspoon paprika

• ¼ teaspoon ground black pepper

Preparation

1- Brush each fillet with butter.

2- Combine the rest of the ingredients in a small bowl, then rub them on the fish. Place the fillets in the deep fryer basket.

3- Set the temperature to 390 ° F and set the timer to 7 minutes.

4- Once the cooking is complete, the internal temperature will be 145 ° F. Serve immediately.

Nutrition facts per serving

Calories: 253

Fat: 16.6 g

Protein: 20.9 g

Carb: 1 g

Fiber: 0.4 g

Cilantro Lime Baked Salmon

Hands-On Time: **10 minutes**; *Cook Time:* **12 minutes**; *Yield*: **2 servings**.

Ingredients

• 2 (3-ounce) salmon fillets, skin removed

• 1 tablespoon salted butter, melted

• 1 teaspoon chili powder

• ½ teaspoon finely minced garlic

• ¼ cup sliced pickled jalapeños

• ½ medium lime juiced

• 2 tablespoons chopped cilantro

Preparation

1- Place the salmon fillets in a 6-inch baking dish. Brush each with butter and sprinkle with chili powder and garlic.

2- Place the slices of jalapeño on top and around the salmon. Pour half of the lime juice over the salmon and cover with foil. Place the pan in the basket of the fryer.

3- Set the temperature to 370 ° F and set the timer to 12 minutes.

4- Once cooked, the salmon should flake easily with the fork and reach an internal temperature of at least 145 ° F.

5- To serve, add the lime juice and garnish with coriander.

Nutrition facts per serving

Calories: 167

Fat: 9.9 g

Protein: 15.8 g

Carb: 0.9 g

Fiber: 0.7 g

Simple Buttery Cod

Hands-On Time: **5 minutes**; *Cook Time:* **8 minutes**; *Yield*: **2 servings**.

Ingredients

- 2 (4-ounce) cod fillets

- 2 tablespoons salted butter, melted

- 1 teaspoon Old Bay seasoning

- ½ medium lemon sliced

Preparation

1- Place the cod fillets in a 6-inch round baking dish. Brush each fillet with butter and sprinkle with Old Bay seasoning. Arrange two slices of lemon on each fillet. Cover the dish with aluminum foil and place it in the basket of the air fryer.

2- Set the temperature to 350 ° F and set the timer to 8 minutes.

3- Return to mid-cooking. Once cooked, the internal temperature should be at least 145 ° F. Serve hot.

Nutrition facts per serving

Calories: 179

Fat: 11.1 g

Protein: 17.4 g

Carb: 0 g

Fiber: 0 g

Sesame-Crusted Tuna Steak

Hands-On Time: **5 minutes**; *Cook Time:* **8 minutes**; *Yield*: **2 servings**.

Ingredients

- 2 (6-ounce) tuna steaks
- 1 tablespoon coconut oil, melted
- ½ teaspoon garlic powder
- 2 teaspoons white sesame seeds
- 2 teaspoons black sesame seeds

Preparation

1- Brush each tuna fillet with coconut oil and sprinkle with garlic powder.

2- In a large bowl, combine the sesame seeds, then squeeze each tuna steak, covering the steak as completely as possible. Place the tuna steaks in the deep fryer basket.

3- Set the temperature to 400 ° F and set the timer to 8 minutes.

4- Turn the steaks halfway through cooking. The steaks will be well cooked at an internal temperature of 145 ° F. Serve hot.

Nutrition facts per serving

Calories: 280

Fat: 10 g

Protein: 42.7 g

Carb: 1.2 g

Fiber: 0.8 g

Lemon Garlic Shrimp

Hands-On Time: **5 minutes**; *Cook Time:* **6 minutes**; *Yield*: **2 servings**.

Ingredients

- 1 medium lemon

- 8 ounces medium shelled and deveined shrimp

- 2 tablespoons unsalted butter, melted

- ½ teaspoon Old Bay seasoning

- ½ teaspoon minced garlic

Preparation

1- zest of lemon then cut in half. Place the shrimp in a large bowl and squeeze the juice of half a lemon on it.

2- Add the lemon peel to the bowl with the rest of the ingredients. Mix the shrimp until they are well coated.

3- Pour the contents of the bowl into a 6-inch round baking dish. Place in the basket of the air fryer.

4- Set the temperature to 400 ° F and set the timer to 6 minutes.

5- The shrimps will be bright pink at the end of cooking. Serve hot with a sauce in the pan.

Nutrition facts per serving

Calories: 190

Fat: 11.8 g

Protein: 16.4 g

Carb: 2.5 g

Fiber: 0.4 g

Firecracker Shrimp

Hands-On Time: **10 minutes**; *Cook Time:* **7 minutes**; *Yield*: **4 servings**.

Ingredients

- 1 pound medium shelled and deveined shrimp

- 2 tablespoons salted butter, melted

- ½ teaspoon Old Bay seasoning

- ¼ teaspoon garlic powder

- 2 tablespoons sriracha

- ¼ teaspoon powdered erythritol

- ¼ cup full-fat mayonnaise

- ⅛ teaspoon ground black pepper

Preparation

1- In a large bowl, combine the butter prawns, Old Bay seasoning and garlic powder. Place the shrimp in the deep fryer basket.

2- Set the temperature to 400 ° F and set the timer to 7 minutes.

3- Turn the shrimp over halfway through cooking. The shrimps will be bright pink at the end of cooking.

4- In another large bowl, mix sriracha, erythritol powder, mayonnaise and pepper. Mix the shrimp with the spicy mixture and serve immediately.

Nutrition facts per serving

Calories: 143

Fat: 6.4 g

Protein: 16.4 g

Carb: 2.8 g

Fiber: 0 g

Blackened Shrimp

Hands-On Time: **5 minutes**; *Cook Time:* **6 minutes**; *Yield*: **2 servings**.

Ingredients

- 8 ounces medium shelled and deveined shrimp

- 2 tablespoons salted butter, melted

- 1 teaspoon paprika

- ½ teaspoon garlic powder

- ¼ teaspoon onion powder

- ½ teaspoon Old Bay seasoning

Preparation

1- Mix all ingredients in a large bowl. Place the shrimp in the deep fryer basket.

2- Set the temperature to 400 ° F and set the timer to 6 minutes.

3- Turn the shrimp halfway through cooking to ensure even cooking. Serve immediately.

Nutrition facts per serving

Calories: 192

Fat: 11.9 g

Protein: 16.6 g

Carb: 2 g

Fiber: 0.5 g

<u>Coconut Shrimp</u>

Hands-On Time: **5 minutes**; *Cook Time:* **6 minutes**; *Yield*: **2 servings**.

Ingredients

• 8 ounces medium shelled and deveined shrimp

• 2 tablespoons salted butter, melted

• ½ teaspoon Old Bay seasoning

• ¼ cup unsweetened shredded coconut

Preparation

1- In a large bowl, combine Old Bay Butter and Seasoning Shrimp.

2- Place the grated coconut in a bowl. Coat each piece of shrimp in the coconut and place it in the basket of the fryer.

3- Set the temperature to 400 ° F and set the timer to 6 minutes.

4- Turn the shrimp gently halfway through cooking. Serve immediately.

Nutrition facts per serving

Calories: 252

Fat: 17.8 g

Protein: 16.9 g

Carb: 1.8 g

Fiber: 2 g

Tuna Zoodle Casserole

Hands-On Time: **15 minutes**; *Cook Time:* **15 minutes**; *Yield:* **4 servings**.

Ingredients

• 2 tablespoons salted butter

• ¼ cup diced white onion

• ¼ cup chopped white mushrooms

• 2 stalks celery, finely chopped

• ½ cup heavy cream

• ½ cup vegetable broth

• 2 tablespoons full-fat mayonnaise

• ¼ teaspoon xanthan gum

• ½ teaspoon red pepper flakes

• 2 medium zucchini spiraled

• 2 (5-ounce) can albacore tuna

• 1 ounce pork rinds, finely ground

Preparation

1- In a large saucepan over medium heat, melt the butter; Add onion, mushrooms and celery and sauté for about 3 to 5 minutes until fragrant.

2- Pour thick cream, vegetable broth, mayonnaise and xanthan gum. Reduce the heat and continue cooking for another 3 minutes, until the mixture starts to thicken.

3- Add the red pepper flakes, zucchini and tuna. Turn off the heat and stir until zucchini noodles are coated.

4- Pour into a round baking dish of 4 cups. Garnish chopped pork rinds and cover the top of the dish with foil. Place in the basket of the air fryer.

5- Set the temperature to 370 ° F and set the timer to 15 minutes.

6- When there are only 3 minutes left, remove the foil to brown the top of the pan. Serve hot.

Nutrition facts per serving

Calories: 339; Fat: 25.1 g; Protein: 19.7 g; Carb: 4.3 g; Fiber: 1.8 g

Foil-Packet Salmon

Hands-On Time: **10 minutes**; *Cook Time:* **12 minutes**; *Yield*: **2 servings**.

Ingredients

• 2 (4-ounce) salmon fillets, skin removed

• 2 tablespoons unsalted butter, melted

• ½ teaspoon garlic powder

• 1 medium lemon

• ½ teaspoon dried dill

Preparation

1- Place each net on a square of 5 × 5-inch aluminum foil. Sprinkle with butter and sprinkle with garlic powder.

2- Zest half of the lemon and sprinkle the zest over the salmon. Slice the other half of the lemon and place two slices on each piece of salmon. Sprinkle dill over salmon.

3- Gather and fold the film at the top and sides to completely close the packages. Place the aluminum packets in the basket of the air fryer.

4- Set the temperature to 400 ° F and set the timer to 12 minutes.

5- Salmon will be easily crumbled and its internal temperature will be at least 145 ° F when fully cooked. Serve immediately.

Nutrition facts per serving

Calories: 252

Fat: 16.5 g

Protein: 2.9 g

Carb: 0.8 g

Fiber: 0.4 g

Crispy Fish Sticks

Hands-On Time: **15 minutes**; *Cook Time:* **10 minutes**; *Yield*: **4 servings**.

Ingredients

- 1 ounce pork rinds, finely ground

- ¼ cup blanched finely ground almond flour

- ½ teaspoon Old Bay seasoning

- 1 tablespoon coconut oil

- 1 large egg

- 1 pound cod fillet, cut into ¾-inch strips

Preparation

1- In large bowl, combine chopped pork rinds, almond flour, Old Bay seasoning and coconut oil and mix. In a medium bowl, whisk the egg.

2- Dip each fish stick into the egg, then gently press the flour mixture, wrapping it as completely and as evenly as possible. Place the fish sticks in the basket of the air fryer.

3- Set the temperature to 400 ° F and set the timer to 10 minutes or until the colors are golden.

4- Serve immediately.

Nutrition facts per serving

Calories: 205

Fat: 10.7 g

Protein: 24.4 g

Carb: 0.8 g

Fiber: 0.8 g

Foil-Packet Lobster Tail

Hands-On Time: **15 minutes**; *Cook Time:* **12 minutes**; *Yield*: **2 servings**.

Ingredients

• 2 (6-ounce) lobster tails halved

• 2 tablespoons salted butter, melted

• ½ teaspoon Old Bay seasoning

• Juice of ½ medium lemon

• 1 teaspoon dried parsley

Preparation

1- Place the two tails cut in half on a sheet of aluminum foil. Drizzle with butter, Old Bay seasoning and lemon juice.

2- Seal the aluminum packets by completely covering the tails. Place in the basket of the air fryer.

3- Set the temperature to 375 ° F and set the timer to 12 minutes.

4- Once cooked, sprinkle with dried parsley and serve immediately.

Nutrition facts per serving

Calories: 234

Fat: 11.9 g

Protein: 28.3 g

Carb: 0.6 g

Fiber: 0.1 g

Fried Tuna Salad Bites

Hands-On Time: **10 minutes**; *Cook Time:* **7 minutes**; *Yield*: **12 bites**.

Ingredients

- 1 (10-ounce) can tuna, drained

- ¼ cup full-fat mayonnaise

- 1 stalk celery, chopped

- 1 medium avocado, peeled, pitted, and mashed

- ½ cup blanched finely ground almond flour, divided

- 2 teaspoons coconut oil

Preparation

1- In a large bowl, combine tuna, mayonnaise, celery and avocado puree. Form the mixture into balls.

2- Roll the balls in almond flour and spritz in coconut oil. Place the balls in the basket of the fryer.

3- Set the temperature to 400 ° F and set the timer to 7 minutes.

4- Turn the tuna bites gently after 5 minutes. Serve hot.

Nutrition facts per serving

Calories: 323

Fat: 25.4 g

Protein: 17.3 g

Carb: 2.3 g

Fiber: 4 g

Fish Taco Bowl with Jalapeño Slaw

Hands-On Time: **10 minutes**; *Cook Time:* **10 minutes***; Yield*: **2 servings**.

Ingredients

- 1 cup shredded cabbage
- ¼ cup full-fat sour cream
- 2 tablespoons full-fat mayonnaise
- ¼ cup chopped pickled jalapeños
- 2 (3-ounce) cod fillets
- 1 teaspoon chili powder
- 1 teaspoon cumin
- ½ teaspoon paprika
- ¼ teaspoon garlic powder
- 1 medium avocado, peeled, pitted, and sliced
- ½ medium lime

Preparation

1- In a large bowl, put the cabbage, sour cream, mayonnaise and jalapeños. Mix until completely coated. Let stand for 20 minutes in the refrigerator.

2- Sprinkle the cod fillets with chili powder, cumin, paprika and garlic powder. Place each fillet in the basket of the air fryer.

3- Set the temperature to 370 ° F and set the timer to 10 minutes.

4- Turn the fillets halfway through cooking. Once cooked, the fish must have an internal temperature of at least 145 ° F.

5- To serve, divide the cabbage salad mix into two bowls, cut the cod fillets into pieces, spread them over the bowls and cover with avocado. Squeeze the lime juice on each bowl. Serve immediately.

Nutrition facts per serving

Calories: 342; Fat: 25.2 g; Protein: 16.1 g; Carb: 5.3 g; Fiber: 6.4 g

VEGETARIAN MAIN DISHES

Although meats are an easy way to get the essential protein for a healthy ketogenic diet, vegetables are also very important to make sure you're well fed. And the air fryer is definitely for something other than cooking meat! These vegetarian main courses are perfect if you try a meatless Monday or simply get your protein from a source other than meat.

Quiche-Stuffed Peppers

Hands-On Time: **5 minutes**; *Cook Time:* **15 minutes**; *Yield*: **2 servings**.

Ingredients

• 2 green bell peppers

• 3 large eggs

• ¼ cup full-fat ricotta cheese

• ¼ cup diced yellow onion

• ½ cup chopped broccoli

• ½ cup shredded medium Cheddar cheese

Preparation

1- Cut the peppers off the top and remove the pips and white membranes with a small knife.

2- In a medium bowl, whisk together eggs and ricotta.

3- Add the onion and broccoli. Pour the egg and vegetable mixture into each pepper. Garnish with cheddar cheese. Place the peppers in a 4-cup baking dish and place in the deep fryer basket.

4- Set the temperature to 350 ° F and set the timer to 15 minutes.

5- Eggs will usually be firm and peppers soft at the end of cooking. Serve immediately.

Nutrition facts per serving

Calories: 314

Fat: 18.7 g

Protein: 21.6 g

Carb: 7.8 g

Fiber: 3 g

Roasted Garlic White Zucchini Rolls

Hands-On Time: **20 minutes**; *Cook Time:* **20 minutes**; *Yield*: **4 servings**.

Ingredients

- 2 medium zucchini
- 2 tablespoons unsalted butter
- ¼ white onion, peeled and diced
- ½ teaspoon finely minced roasted garlic
- ¼ cup heavy cream
- 2 tablespoons vegetable broth
- ⅛ teaspoon xanthan gum
- ½ cup full-fat ricotta cheese
- ¼ teaspoon salt
- ½ teaspoon garlic powder
- ¼ teaspoon dried oregano
- 2 cups spinach, chopped
- ½ cup sliced baby portobello mushrooms
- ¾ cup shredded mozzarella cheese, divided

Preparation

1- Using a mandoline or sharp knife, cut zucchini into long slices lengthwise. Place the strips between the paper towels to absorb moisture. Put aside.

2- In a medium saucepan over medium heat, melt the butter; Add the onion and sauté until fragrant. Add garlic and sauté 30 seconds.

3- Pour the heavy cream, broth and xanthan gum. Turn off the heat and whisk the mixture until it begins to thicken, about 3 minutes.

4- In a medium bowl, add ricotta, salt, garlic powder and oregano and mix well. Stir in spinach, mushrooms and ½-cup mozzarella.

5- Pour half of the sauce into a 6-inch round baking pan. To assemble the rolls, place two strips of zucchini on a work surface. Spoon 2 tablespoons of ricotta mixture onto the slices and roll up. Place seam side down on top of sauce. Repeat with remaining ingredients.

6- Pour remaining sauce over buns and sprinkle with remaining mozzarella. Cover with foil and place in the basket of the air fryer.

7- Set the temperature to 350 ° F and set the timer to 20 minutes.

8- In the last 5 minutes, remove the leaf to brown the cheese. Serve immediately.

Nutrition facts per serving

Calories: 245

Fat: 18.9 g

Protein: 10.5 g

Carb: 5.3 g

Fiber: 1.8 g

Spicy Parmesan Artichokes

Hands-On Time: **10 minutes**; *Cook Time:* **10 minutes**; *Yield*: **4 servings**.

Ingredients

• 2 medium artichokes, trimmed and quartered, center removed

• 2 tablespoons coconut oil

• 1 large egg, beaten

• ½ cup grated vegetarian Parmesan cheese

• ¼ cup blanched finely ground almond flour

• ½ teaspoon crushed red pepper flakes

Preparation

1- In a large bowl, mix the artichokes in the coconut oil, then dip each piece into the egg.

2- Mix the Parmesan and almond flour in a large bowl. Add the artichoke pieces and mix to cover as completely as possible, sprinkle with chili flakes. Place in the basket of the air fryer.

3- Set the temperature to 400 ° F and set the timer to 10 minutes.

4- Stir the basket twice during cooking. Serve hot.

Nutrition facts per serving

Calories: 189

Fat: 13.5 g

Protein: 7.9 g

Carb: 5.8 g

Fiber: 4.2 g

Broccoli Crust Pizza

Hands-On Time: **15 minutes**; *Cook Time:* **12 minutes**; *Yield*: **4 servings**.

Ingredients

• 3 cups rice broccoli steamed and drained well

• 1 large egg

• ½ cup grated vegetarian Parmesan cheese

• 3 tablespoons low-carb Alfredo sauce

• ½ cup shredded mozzarella cheese

Preparation

1- In a large bowl, combine broccoli, egg and Parmesan cheese.

2- Cut out a piece of parchment suitable for your air fryer basket. Squeeze the pizza mixture into the parchment, working twice, if necessary. Place in the basket of the air fryer.

3- Set the temperature to 370 ° F and set the timer to 5 minutes.

4- When the timer sounds, the crust must be firm enough to rock. Otherwise, add 2 more minutes. Flip the crust.

5- Garnish with Alfredo sauce and mozzarella. Put back in the basket of the fryer and cook another 7 minutes or until the cheese is golden and bubbly. Serve hot.

Nutrition facts per serving

Calories: 136

Fat: 7.6 g

Protein: 9.9 g

Carb: 3.4 g

Fiber: 2.3 g

Crustless Spinach Cheese Pie

Hands-On Time: **10 minutes**; *Cook Time:* **20 minutes**; *Yield*: **4 servings**.

Ingredients

• 6 large eggs

• ¼ cup heavy whipping cream

• 1 cup frozen chopped spinach, drained

• 1 cup shredded sharp Cheddar cheese

• ¼ cup diced yellow onion

Preparation

1- In a medium bowl, beat the eggs and add the cream. Add the remaining ingredients to the bowl.

2- Pour into a 6-inch round baking dish. Place in the basket of the air fryer.

3- Set the temperature to 320 ° F and set the timer to 20 minutes.

4- Eggs will be firm and lightly browned when cooked. Serve immediately.

Nutrition facts per serving

Calories: 288

Fat: 20 g

Protein: 18 g

Carb: 2.6 g

Fiber: 1.3 g

Zucchini Cauliflower Fritters

Hands-On Time: **15 minutes**; *Cook Time:* **12 minutes**; *Yield*: **2 servings**.

Ingredients

- 1 (12-ounce) cauliflower steamer bag
- 1 medium zucchini shredded
- ¼ cup almond flour
- 1 large egg
- ½ teaspoon garlic powder
- ¼ cup grated vegetarian Parmesan cheese

Preparation

1- Cook the cauliflower according to package directions and drain excess moisture in a stamen or paper towel. Place in a large bowl.

2- Place the zucchini in a paper towel and dab to remove excess moisture. Add to bowl with cauliflower. Add remaining ingredients.

3- Spread the mixture evenly and form four patties. Press into patties ¼-inch thick. Place each in the basket of the fryer.

4- Set the temperature to 320 ° F and set the timer to 12 minutes.

5- Fritters will be firm when fully cooked. Allow to cool 5 minutes before moving. Serve hot.

Nutrition facts per serving

Calories: 217

Fat: 12 g

Protein: 13.7 g

Carb: 8.5 g

Fiber: 6.5 g

Loaded Cauliflower Steak

Hands-On Time: **5 minutes**; *Cook Time:* **7 minutes**; *Yield*: **4 servings**.

Ingredients

- 1 medium head cauliflower

- ¼ cup hot sauce

- 2 tablespoons salted butter, melted

- ¼ cup blue cheese crumbles

- ¼ cup full-fat ranch dressing

Preparation

1- Remove the cauliflower leaves. Slice the head into ½-inch-thick slices.

2- In a small bowl, combine the hot sauce and butter. Brush the mixture on the cauliflower.

3- Place each cauliflower steak in the air fryer, in batches, if necessary.

4- Set the temperature to 400 ° F and set the timer to 7 minutes.

5- Once cooked, the edges will turn dark and caramelized.

6- To serve, sprinkle blue cheese steaks crumbled. Sprinkle with ranch vinaigrette.

Nutrition facts per serving

Calories: 122

Fat: 8.4 g

Protein: 4.9 g

Carb: 4.7 g

Fiber: 3 g

Cheesy Zoodle Bake

Hands-On Time: **10 minutes**; *Cook Time:* **8 minutes**; *Yield*: **4 servings**.

Ingredients

- 2 tablespoons salted butter

- ¼ cup diced white onion

- ½ teaspoon minced garlic

- ½ cup heavy whipping cream

- 2 ounces full-fat cream cheese

- 1 cup shredded sharp Cheddar cheese

- 2 medium zucchini spiraled

Preparation

1- In a large saucepan over medium heat, melt the butter; Add onion and sauté until softened, 1 to 3 minutes. Add the garlic and sauté 30 seconds then pour the cream and add the cream cheese.

2- Remove the pan from the heat and stir in the cheddar cheese. Add the zucchini and stir in the sauce, then pour into a round baking dish of 4 cups. Cover the dish with aluminum foil and place it in the basket of the air fryer.

3- Set the temperature to 370 ° F and set the timer to 8 minutes.

4- After 6 minutes, remove the foil and let the top brown for the remaining cooking time. Stir and serve.

Nutrition facts per serving

Calories: 337

Fat: 28.4 g

Protein: 9.6 g

Carb: 4.7 g

Fiber: 1.2 g

Greek Stuffed Eggplant

Hands-On Time: **15 minutes**; *Cook Time:* **20 minutes**; *Yield*: **2 servings**.

Ingredients

- 1 large eggplant
- 2 tablespoons unsalted butter
- ¼ medium yellow onion, diced
- ¼ cup chopped artichoke hearts
- 1 cup fresh spinach
- 2 tablespoons diced red bell pepper
- ½ cup crumbled feta

Preparation

1- Slice eggplant in half lengthwise and remove the flesh leaving enough room inside to keep the shell intact. Take the picked eggplants, chop them and set them aside.

2- In a medium skillet over medium heat, add the butter and onion. Sauté until the onions begin to soften, about 3 to 5 minutes. Add chopped eggplant, artichokes, spinach and chopped pepper. Continue cooking for 5 minutes until the peppers are soft and the spinach fades; Remove from heat and gently stir in the feta cheese.

3- Place the filling in each eggplant shell and place it in the basket of the air fryer.

4- Set the temperature to 320 ° F and set the timer to 20 minutes.

5- Eggplant will be tender when finished. Serve hot.

Nutrition facts per serving

Calories: 291

Fat: 18.7 g

Protein: 9.4 g

Carb: 11.8 g

Fiber: 10.8 g

Roasted Broccoli Salad

Hands-On Time: **10 minutes**; *Cook Time:* **7 minutes**; *Yield*: **2 servings**.

Ingredients

- 3 cups fresh broccoli florets

- 2 tablespoons salted butter, melted

- ¼ cup sliced almonds

- ½ medium lemon

Preparation

1- Place the broccoli in a 6-inch round baking dish. Pour the butter over the broccoli. Add the almonds and mix. Place the dish in the basket of the fryer.

2- Set the temperature to 380 ° F and set the timer to 7 minutes.

3- Blend halfway through cooking.

4- When the timer rings sprinkle the lemon on the broccoli and press the juice into the mold. Launch. Serve hot.

Nutrition facts per serving

Calories: 215

Fat: 16.3 g

Protein: 6.4 g

Carb: 7.1 g

Fiber: 5 g

<u>Basic Spaghetti Squash</u>

Hands-On Time: **10 minutes**; *Cook Time:* **45 minutes**; *Yield*: **2 servings**.

Ingredients

- ½ large spaghetti squash

- 1 tablespoon coconut oil

- 2 tablespoons salted butter, melted

- ½ teaspoon garlic powder

- 1 teaspoon dried parsley

Preparation

1- Brush the spaghetti squash shell with coconut oil. Place the skin side down and brush the inside with butter. Sprinkle with garlic powder and parsley.

2- Place the squash, skin down, in the deep fryer basket.

3- Set the temperature to 350 ° F and set the timer to 30 minutes.

4- When the timer rings turn the squash so that the skin is up and cook another 15 minutes or until the fork is tender. Serve hot.

Nutrition facts per serving

Calories: 182

Fat: 11.7 g

Protein: 1.9 g

Carb: 14.3 g

Fiber: 3.9 g

Three-Cheese Zucchini Boats

Hands-On Time: **15 minutes**; *Cook Time:* **20 minutes**; *Yield:* **2 servings**.

Ingredients

• 2 medium zucchini

• 1 tablespoon avocado oil

• ¼ cup low-carb, no-sugar-added pasta sauce

• ¼ cup full-fat ricotta cheese

• ¼ cup shredded mozzarella cheese

• ¼ teaspoon dried oregano

• ¼ teaspoon garlic powder

• ½ teaspoon dried parsley

• 2 tablespoons grated vegetarian Parmesan cheese

Preparation

1- Cut 1 inch from the top and bottom of each zucchini. Cut the zucchini in half lengthwise and use a spoon to remove some of the inside, which will allow you to stuff them. Brush with oil and pour 2 tablespoons of pasta sauce into each shell.

2- In a medium bowl, combine ricotta, mozzarella, oregano, garlic powder and parsley. Pour the mixture into each zucchini shell. Place the stuffed zucchini in the deep fryer basket.

3- Set the temperature to 350 ° F and set the timer to 20 minutes.

4- To remove the basket from the deep fryer, use a pair of pliers or spatula and lift gently. Garnish with Parmesan cheese. Serve immediately.

Nutrition facts per serving

Calories: 215

Fat: 14.9 g

Protein: 10.5 g

Carb: 6.6 g

Fiber: 2.7 g

Spinach Artichoke Casserole

Hands-On Time: **15 minutes**; *Cook Time:* **15 minutes**; *Yield:* **4 servings**.

Ingredients

- 1 tablespoon salted butter, melted

- ¼ cup diced yellow onion

- 8 ounces full-fat cream cheese, softened

- ⅓ cup full-fat mayonnaise

- ⅓ cup full-fat sour cream

- ¼ cup chopped pickled jalapeños

- 2 cups fresh spinach, chopped

- 2 cups cauliflower florets chopped

- 1 cup artichoke hearts chopped

Preparation

1- In a large bowl, combine butter, onion, cream cheese, mayonnaise and sour cream. Stir in jalapeños, spinach, cauliflower and artichokes.

2- Pour the mixture into a round baking dish of 4 cups. Cover with foil and place in the basket of the air fryer.

3- Set the temperature to 370 ° F and set the timer to 15 minutes.

4- During the last 2 minutes of cooking, remove the foil to brown the top. Serve hot.

Nutrition facts per serving

Calories: 423

Fat: 36.3 g

Protein: 6.7 g

Carb: 6.8 g

Fiber: 5.3 g

Portobello Mini Pizzas

Hands-On Time: **10 minutes**; *Cook Time:* **10 minutes**; *Yield:* **2 servings**.

Ingredients

- 2 large portobello mushrooms

- 2 tablespoons unsalted butter, melted

- ½ teaspoon garlic powder

- ⅔ cup shredded mozzarella cheese

- 4 grape tomatoes sliced

- 2 leaves fresh basil, chopped

- 1 tablespoon balsamic vinegar

Preparation

1- Pick up the inside of the mushrooms leaving only the caps. Brush each cap with butter and sprinkle with garlic powder.

2- Fill each bonnet with mozzarella and tomato slices. Place each mini-pizza in a 6-inch round dish. Place the pan in the basket of the fryer.

3- Set the temperature to 380 ° F and set the timer to 10 minutes.

4- Carefully remove the pizzas from the fryer basket and garnish with basil and a drizzle of vinegar.

Nutrition facts per serving

Calories: 244

Fat: 18.5 g

Protein: 10.4 g

Carb: 5.4 g

Fiber: 1.4 g

Veggie Quesadilla

Hands-On Time: **10 minutes**; *Cook Time:* **5 minutes**; *Yield*: **2 servings**.

Ingredients

- 1 tablespoon coconut oil
- ½ green bell pepper, seeded and chopped
- ¼ cup diced red onion
- ¼ cup chopped white mushrooms
- 4 flatbread dough tortillas
- ⅔ cup shredded pepper jack cheese
- ½ medium avocado, peeled, pitted, and mashed
- ¼ cup full-fat sour cream
- ¼ cup mild salsa

Preparation

1- In a medium skillet over medium heat, heat the coconut oil. Add the pepper, onion and mushrooms in the pan and sauté until the peppers begin to soften, 3 to 5 minutes.

2- Place two tortillas on a work surface and sprinkle each on half of the cheese. Garnish with sautéed vegetables, sprinkle with remaining cheese and place the other two tortillas on top. Carefully place the quesadillas in the basket of the air fryer.

3- Set the temperature to 400 ° F and set the timer to 5 minutes.

4- Return the quesadillas halfway through cooking. Serve hot with avocado, sour cream and salsa.

Nutrition facts per serving

Calories: 795

Fat: 61.3 g

Protein: 34.5 g

Carb: 12.9 g

Fiber: 6.5 g

Roasted Veggie Bowl

Hands-On Time: **10 minutes**; *Cook Time:* **15 minutes**; *Yield:* **2 servings**.

Ingredients

- 1 cup broccoli florets
- 1 cup quartered Brussels sprouts
- ½ cup cauliflower florets
- ¼ medium white onion, peeled and sliced ¼-inch thick
- ½ green bell pepper, seeded and sliced ¼-inch thick
- 1 tablespoon coconut oil
- 2 teaspoons chili powder
- ½ teaspoon garlic powder
- ½ teaspoon cumin

Preparation

1- Mix all ingredients in a large bowl until vegetables are completely covered with oil and seasoning.

2- Pour the vegetables into the basket of the air fryer.

3- Set the temperature to 360 ° F and set the timer to 15 minutes.

4- Shake two or three times while cooking. Serve hot.

Nutrition facts per serving

Calories: 121

Fat: 7.1 g

Protein: 4.3 g

Carb: 7.9 g

Fiber: 5.2 g

Spaghetti Squash Alfredo

Hands-On Time: **10 minutes**; *Cook Time:* **15 minutes**; *Yield*: **2 servings**.

Ingredients

- ½ large cooked spaghetti squash
- 2 tablespoons salted butter, melted
- ½ cup low-carb Alfredo sauce
- ¼ cup grated vegetarian Parmesan cheese
- ½ teaspoon garlic powder
- 1 teaspoon dried parsley
- ¼ teaspoon ground peppercorn
- ½ cup shredded Italian blend cheese

Preparation

1- Using a fork, remove the spaghetti squash pieces from the hull. Place in a large bowl with butter and Alfredo sauce. Sprinkle with Parmesan cheese, garlic powder, parsley and pepper.

2- Pour in a round baking dish of 4 cups and garnish with grated cheese. Place the dish in the basket of the fryer.

3- Set the temperature to 320 ° F and set the timer to 15 minutes.

4- Once finished, the cheese will be golden and bubbling. Serve immediately.

Nutrition facts per serving

Calories: 375

Fat: 24.2 g

Protein: 13.5 g

Carb: 20.1 g

Fiber: 4 g

Caprese Eggplant Stacks

Hands-On Time: **5 minutes**; *Cook Time:* **12 minutes**; *Yield:* **4 servings**.

Ingredients

- 1 medium eggplant, cut into ¼-inch slices

- 2 large tomatoes, cut into ¼-inch slices

- 4 ounces fresh mozzarella cut into ½-ounce slices

- 2 tablespoons olive oil

- ¼ cup fresh basil sliced

Preparation

1- In a 6-inch baking dish, place four eggplant slices on the bottom. Place a slice of tomato on each eggplant turn, then mozzarella and eggplant. Repeat if necessary.

2- Sprinkle with olive oil. Cover the dish with aluminum foil and place it in the basket of the air fryer.

3- Set the temperature to 350 ° F and set the timer to 12 minutes.

4- Once finished, the eggplant will be tender. Garnish with fresh basil to serve.

Nutrition facts per serving

Calories: 195

Fat: 12.7 g

Protein: 8.5 g

Carb: 7.5 g

Fiber: 5.2 g

Cheesy Cauliflower Pizza Crust

Hands-On Time: **15 minutes**; *Cook Time:* **11 minutes**; *Yield*: **2 servings**.

Ingredients

• 1 (12-ounce) steamer bag cauliflower

• ½ cup shredded sharp Cheddar cheese

• 1 large egg

• 2 tablespoons blanched finely ground almond flour

• 1 teaspoon Italian blend seasoning

Preparation

1- Cook the cauliflower according to the directions on the package. Remove from the bag and place in a cheesecloth or paper towel to remove excess water. Place the cauliflower in a large bowl.

2- Add the cheese, egg, almond flour and Italian seasoning to the bowl and mix well.

3- Cut out a piece of parchment suitable for your air fryer basket. Squeeze the cauliflower in a 6-inch circle. Place in the basket of the air fryer.

4- Set the temperature to 360 ° F and set the timer to 11 minutes.

5- After 7 minutes, turn over the pizza crust.

6- Add the favorite toppings to the pizza. Return to the fryer basket and cook another 4 minutes or until completely cooked and browned. Serve immediately.

Nutrition facts per serving

Calories: 230

Fat: 14.2 g

Protein: 14.9 g

Carb: 5.3 g

Fiber: 4.7 g

Italian Baked Egg and Veggies

Hands-On Time: **10 minutes**; *Cook Time:* **10 minutes**; *Yield:* **2 servings**.

Ingredients

- 2 tablespoons salted butter
- 1 small zucchini sliced lengthwise and quartered
- ½ green bell pepper, seeded and diced
- 1 cup fresh spinach, chopped
- 1 medium Roma tomato, diced
- 2 large eggs
- ¼ teaspoon onion powder
- ¼ teaspoon garlic powder
- ½ teaspoon dried basil
- ¼ teaspoon dried oregano

Preparation

1- Grease two ramekins with 1 tablespoon of butter each.

2- In a large bowl, combine zucchini, peppers, spinach and tomatoes. Divide the mixture in half and place half in each ramekin.

3- Break one egg over each ramekin and sprinkle with powdered onion, garlic powder, basil and oregano. Place in the basket of the air fryer.

4- Set the temperature to 330 ° F and set the timer to 10 minutes.

5- Serve immediately.

Nutrition facts per serving

Calories: 150

Fat: 10 g

Protein: 8.3 g

Carb: 4.4 g

Fiber: 2.2 g

BBQ Pulled Mushrooms

Hands-On Time: **5 minutes**; *Cook Time:* **12 minutes**; *Yield*: **2 servings**.

Ingredients

• 4 large portobello mushrooms

• 1 tablespoon salted butter, melted

• ¼ teaspoon ground black pepper

• 1 teaspoon chili powder

• 1 teaspoon paprika

• ¼ teaspoon onion powder

• ½ cup low-carb, sugar-free barbecue sauce

Preparation

1- Remove the stem and hollow out the underside of each fungus. Brush the caps with butter and sprinkle with pepper, chili powder, paprika and onion powder.

2- Place the mushrooms in the basket of the air fryer.

3- Set the temperature to 400 ° F and set the timer to 8 minutes.

4- When the timer sounds remove the mushrooms from the basket and place them on a cutting board or on a work surface. Using two forks, gently separate the mushrooms by creating strands.

5- Place the mushroom sprigs in a round 4-cup baking dish with the barbecue sauce. Place the dish in the basket of the fryer.

6- Set the temperature to 350 ° F and set the timer to 4 minutes.

7- Blend halfway through cooking. Serve hot.

Nutrition facts per serving

Calories: 108

Fat: 5.9 g

Protein: 3.3 g

Carb: 8.2 g

Fiber: 2.7 g

Whole Roasted Lemon Cauliflower

Hands-On Time: **6 minutes**; *Cook Time:* **15 minutes**; *Yield*: **4 servings**.

Ingredients

- 1 medium head cauliflower

- 2 tablespoons salted butter, melted

- 1 medium lemon

- ½ teaspoon garlic powder

- 1 teaspoon dried parsley

Preparation

1- Remove the leaves from the head of the cauliflower and brush with melted butter. Cut the lemon in half and zip one half on the cauliflower. Squeeze the juice of half of lemon zest and pour it over the cauliflower.

2- Sprinkle with garlic powder and parsley. Place the cauliflower head in the basket of the air fryer.

3- Set the temperature to 350 ° F and set the timer to 15 minutes.

4- Check the cauliflower every 5 minutes to avoid overcooking. It should be a fork.

5- To serve, squeeze the juice of half a lemon on the cauliflower. Serve immediately.

Nutrition facts per serving

Calories: 91

Fat: 5.7 g

Protein: 3 g

Carb: 5.2 g

Fiber: 3.2 g

DESSERTS

Desserts are usually the most difficult thing to give up for any type of diet. Fortunately, there are tons of keto-friendly options to keep you on track while keeping your sweet tooth satisfied! With your air fryer, you can create a wide range of perfectly dosed treats that always fall on stage! As a bonus, with the cooking chamber smaller than a traditional oven, these also treat cook very quickly! From espresso chocolate mini cake to caramel monkey bread, this chapter contains enough treats to make sure you never feel helpless!

Blackberry Crisp

Hands-On Time: **6 minutes**; *Cook Time:* **15 minutes**; *Yield*: **4 servings**.

Ingredients

• 2 cups blackberries

• ⅓ cup powdered erythritol

• 2 tablespoons lemon juice

• ¼ teaspoon xanthan gum

• 1 cup Crunchy Granola

Preparation

1- In a large bowl, combine blackberries, erythritol, lemon juice and xanthan gum.

2- Pour into a 6-inch round baking dish and cover with foil. Place in the basket of the air fryer.

3- Set the temperature to 350 ° F and set the timer to 12 minutes.

4- When the timer sounds remove the movie and stir.

5- Sprinkle the granola on the mixture and return to the basket of the air fryer.

6- Set the temperature to 320 ° F and set the timer to 3 minutes or until the top is golden brown.

7- Serve hot.

Nutrition facts per serving

Calories: 496

Fat: 42.1 g

Protein: 9.2 g

Carb: 9.7 g

Fiber: 12.5 g

Toasted Coconut Flakes

Hands-On Time: **5 minutes**; *Cook Time:* **3 minutes**; *Yield*: **4 servings**.

Ingredients

• 1 cup unsweetened coconut flakes

• 2 teaspoons coconut oil

• ¼ cup granular erythritol

• ⅛ teaspoon salt

Preparation

1- Mix the coconut flakes and oil in a large bowl until well coated. Sprinkle with erythritol and salt.

2- Place the coconut flakes in the basket of the air fryer.

3- Set the temperature to 300 ° F and set the timer to 3 minutes.

4- Mix the flakes when there is only one minute left. Add an extra minute if you want a more golden coconut flake.

Nutrition facts per serving

Calories: 165

Fat: 15.5 g

Protein: 1.3 g

Carb: 2.6 g

Fiber: 2.7 g

Chocolate Mayo Cake

Hands-On Time: **10 minutes**; *Cook Time:* **25 minutes**; *Yield*: **6 servings**.

Ingredients

- 1 cup blanched finely ground almond flour

- ¼ cup salted butter, melted

- ½ cup plus 1 tablespoon granular erythritol

- 1 teaspoon vanilla extract

- ¼ cup full-fat mayonnaise

- ¼ cup unsweetened cocoa powder

- 2 large eggs

Preparation

1- In a large bowl, combine all ingredients until smooth.

2- Pour the dough into a 6-inch round pan. Place in the basket of the air fryer.

3- Set the temperature to 300 ° F and set the timer to 25 minutes.

4- Once finished, a toothpick inserted in the center will come out clean. Let the cake cool completely, otherwise it will collapse once moved.

Nutrition facts per serving

Calories: 270

Fat: 25.1 g

Protein: 7 g

Carb: 3 g

Fiber: 3.3 g

Vanilla Pound Cake

Hands-On Time: **10 minutes**; *Cook Time:* **25 minutes**; *Yield*: **6 servings**.

Ingredients

• 1 cup blanched finely ground almond flour

• ¼ cup salted butter, melted

• ½ cup granular erythritol

• 1 teaspoon vanilla extract

• 1 teaspoon baking powder

• ½ cup full-fat sour cream

• 1 ounce full-fat cream cheese, softened

• 2 large eggs

Preparation

1- In a large bowl, mix almond flour, butter and erythritol.

2- Add vanilla, baking powder, sour cream and cream cheese and mix well. Add the eggs and mix.

3- Pour the dough into a 6-inch round pan. Place the pan in the basket of the fryer.

4- Set the temperature to 300 ° F and set the timer to 25 minutes.

5- Once the cake is cooked, a toothpick inserted in the center will come out clean. The center should not feel wet. Let it cool completely, otherwise the cake will crumble once moved.

Nutrition facts per serving

Calories: 253

Fat: 22.6 g

Protein: 6.9 g

Carb: 3.2 g

Fiber: 2 g

Raspberry Danish Bites

Hands-On Time: **30 minutes**; *Cook Time:* **7 minutes**; *Yield*: **10 servings**.

Ingredients

• 1 cup blanched finely ground almond flour

• 1 teaspoon baking powder

• 3 tablespoons granular Swerve

• 2 ounces full-fat cream cheese, softened

• 1 large egg

• 10 teaspoons sugar-free raspberry preserves

Preparation

1- Mix all ingredients except canned foods in a large bowl until a moist dough is obtained.

2- Place the bowl in the freezer for 20 minutes until the dough is cold and able to roll into a ball.

3- Roll the dough into ten balls and gently press the center of each ball. Place 1 teaspoon of preserves in the center of each bale.

4- Cut out a piece of parchment suitable for your air fryer basket. Place each Danish mouthful on the parchment by gently pressing to flatten the bottom.

5- Set the temperature to 400 ° F and set the timer to 7 minutes.

6- Let them cool completely before moving them, otherwise they will collapse.

Nutrition facts per serving

Calories: 96

Fat: 7.7 g

Protein: 3.4 g

Carb: 4 g

Fiber: 1.3 g

Cream Cheese Danish

Hands-On Time: **20 minutes**; *Cook Time:* **15 minutes**; *Yield:* **6 servings**.

Ingredients

• ¾ cup blanched finely ground almond flour

• 1 cup shredded mozzarella cheese

• 5 ounces full-fat cream cheese, divided

• 2 large egg yolks

• ¾ cup powdered erythritol, divided

• 2 teaspoons vanilla extract divided

Preparation

1- In a large microwaveable bowl, add almond flour, mozzarella and 1-ounce cream cheese. Mix and microwave for 1 minute.

2- Mix and add the egg yolks in the bowl. Continue stirring until soft dough forms. Add ½-cup of erythritol to the dough and 1 teaspoon of vanilla.

3- Cut out a piece of parchment suitable for your air fryer basket. Wet your hands with warm water and press the dough to obtain a ¼-inch thick rectangle.

4- In a medium bowl, combine remaining cream cheese, erythritol and vanilla. Place this cream cheese mixture on the right half of the dough rectangle. Fold the left side of the dough and press to seal. Place in the basket of the air fryer.

5- Set the temperature to 330 ° F and set the timer to 15 minutes.

6- After 7 minutes, return the Dane.

7- When the timer sounds remove the Danish from the parchment and allow it to cool completely before turning it off.

Nutrition facts per serving

Calories: 185

Fat: 14.5 g

Protein: 7.4 g

Carb: 2.3 g

Fiber: 0.5 g

Almond Butter Cookie Balls

Hands-On Time: **5 minutes**; *Cook Time:* **10 minutes**; *Yield*: **10 balls**.

Ingredients

- 1 cup almond butter

- 1 large egg

- 1 teaspoon vanilla extract

- ¼ cup low-carb protein powder

- ¼ cup powdered erythritol

- ¼ cup shredded unsweetened coconut

- ¼ cup low-carb, sugar-free chocolate chips

- ½ teaspoon ground cinnamon

Preparation

1- In a large bowl, mix the almond butter and egg. Add vanilla, protein powder and erythritol.

2- Stir in coconut, chocolate chips and cinnamon. Roll in 1-inch balls. Place the balls in a 6-inch round pan and place them in the basket of the air fryer.

3- Set the temperature to 320 ° F and set the timer to 10 minutes.

4- Cool completely; Store in an airtight container in the refrigerator for up to 4 days.

Nutrition facts per serving

Calories: 224

Fat: 16 g

Protein: 11.2 g

Carb: 1.3 g

Fiber: 3.6 g

Mini Cheesecake

Hands-On Time: **10 minutes**; *Cook Time:* **15 minutes**; *Yield*: **2 servings**.

Ingredients

- ½ cup walnuts

- 2 tablespoons salted butter

- 2 tablespoons granular erythritol

- 4 ounces full-fat cream cheese, softened

- 1 large egg

- ½ teaspoon vanilla extract

- ⅛ cup powdered erythritol

Preparation

1- Place the nuts, butter and erythritol into a food processor. Pulse until the ingredients stick together and a paste forms.

2- Squeeze the dough into a 4-inch hinged pan, then place the pan in the air fryer basket.

3- Set the temperature to 400 ° F and set the timer to 5 minutes.

4- When the timer rings remove the crust and let cool.

5- In a medium bowl, combine the cream cheese with the egg, vanilla extract and powdered erythritol until a smooth mixture is obtained.

6- Place the mixture on the nut crust in the oven and place in the basket of the air fryer.

7- Set the temperature to 300 ° F and set the timer to 10 minutes.

8- Once cooked, let cool 2 hours before serving.

Nutrition facts per serving

Calories: 531

Fat: 48.3 g

Protein: 11.4 g

Carb: 5.1 g

Fiber: 2.3 g

Cinnamon Sugar Pork Rinds

Hands-On Time: **5 minutes**; *Cook Time:* **5 minutes**; *Yield*: **2 servings**.

Ingredients

- 2 ounces pork rinds

- 2 tablespoons unsalted butter, melted

- ½ teaspoon ground cinnamon

- ¼ cup powdered erythritol

Preparation

1- In a large bowl, combine pork rinds and butter. Sprinkle with cinnamon and erythritol, then mix to coat.

2- Place the pork rinds in the basket of the air fryer.

3- Set the temperature to 400 ° F and set the timer to 5 minutes.

4- Serve immediately.

Nutrition facts per serving

Calories: 264

Fat: 20.8 g

Protein: 16.3 g

Carb: 18.5 g

Fiber: 0.4 g

Pecan Brownies

Hands-On Time: **10 minutes**; *Cook Time:* **20 minutes**; *Yield*: **6 servings**.

Ingredients

- ½ cup blanched finely ground almond flour

- ½ cup powdered erythritol

- 2 tablespoons unsweetened cocoa powder

- ½ teaspoon baking powder

- ¼ cup unsalted butter, softened

- 1 large egg

- ¼ cup chopped pecans

- ¼ cup low-carb, sugar-free chocolate chips

Preparation

1- In a large bowl, mix almond flour, erythritol, cocoa powder and baking powder. Stir in the butter and egg.

2- Incorporate pecans and chocolate chips. Place the mixture in a 6-inch round baking dish. Place the pan in the basket of the fryer.

3- Set the temperature to 300 ° F and set the timer to 20 minutes.

4- Once cooked, a toothpick inserted in the center will come out clean. Allow 20 minutes to cool and firm completely.

Nutrition facts per serving

Calories: 215

Fat: 18.9 g

Protein: 4.2 g

Carb: 2.3 g

Fiber: 2.8 g

Pumpkin Spice Pecans

Hands-On Time: **5 minutes**; *Cook Time:* **6 minutes**; *Yield*: **4 servings**.

Ingredients

- 1 cup whole pecans
- ¼ cup granular erythritol
- 1 large egg white
- ½ teaspoon ground cinnamon
- ½ teaspoon pumpkin pie spice
- ½ teaspoon vanilla extract

Preparation

1- Mix all ingredients in a large bowl until pecans are well coated. Place in the basket of the air fryer.

2- Set the temperature to 300 ° F and set the timer to 6 minutes.

3- Mix two to three times during cooking.

4- Cool completely; Store in an airtight container up to 3 days.

Nutrition facts per serving

Calories: 178

Fat: 17 g

Protein: 3.2 g

Carb: 1.4 g

Fiber: 2.6 g

Protein Powder Doughnut Holes

Hands-On Time: **25 minutes**; *Cook Time:* **6 minutes**; *Yield*: **12 holes**.

Ingredients

- ½ cup blanched finely ground almond flour

- ½ cup low-carb vanilla protein powder

- ½ cup granular erythritol

- ½ teaspoon baking powder

- 1 large egg

- 5 tablespoons unsalted butter, melted

- ½ teaspoon vanilla extract

Preparation

1- Mix all ingredients in a large bowl. Place in the freezer for 20 minutes.

2- Wet your hands with water and roll the dough into twelve balls.

3- Cut out a piece of parchment suitable for your air fryer basket. When working in batches if necessary, place donut holes in the basket of the air fryer above the parchment.

4- Set the temperature to 380 ° F and set the timer to 6 minutes.

5- Tip the donut holes halfway through cooking.

6- Let cool completely before serving.

Nutrition facts per serving

Calories: 221

Fat: 14.3 g

Protein: 19.8 g

Carb: 1.5 g

Fiber: 1.7 g

Chocolate-Covered Maple Bacon

Hands-On Time: **5 minutes**; *Cook Time:* **12 minutes**; *Yield*: **2 servings**.

Ingredients

- 8 slices sugar-free bacon

- 1 tablespoon granular erythritol

- ⅓ cup low-carb, sugar-free chocolate chips

- 1 teaspoon coconut oil

- ½ teaspoon maple extract

Preparation

1- Place the bacon in the fryer basket and sprinkle with erythritol.

2- Set the temperature to 350 ° F and set the timer to 12 minutes.

3- Turn the bacon halfway through cooking. Cook to desire cooking, checking to 9 minutes. (Small air fryers cook much faster.)

4- Once the bacon is cooked, let it cool down.

5- In a small microwave-safe bowl, remove the chocolate chips and coconut oil. Microwave for 30 seconds and stir. Add to the maple extract.

6- Place the bacon on a sheet of parchment. Sprinkle the chocolate bacon and put in the refrigerator to cool and harden, about 5 minutes.

Nutrition facts per serving

Calories: 379

Fat: 25.9 g

Protein: 15.3 g

Carb: 3 g

Fiber: 2.7 g

Chocolate Espresso Mini Cheesecake

Hands-On Time: **5 minutes**; *Cook Time:* **15 minutes**; *Yield*: **2 servings**.

Ingredients

- ½ cup walnuts

- 2 tablespoons salted butter

- 2 tablespoons granular erythritol

- 4 ounces full-fat cream cheese, softened

- 1 large egg

- ½ teaspoon vanilla extract

- 2 tablespoons powdered erythritol

- 2 teaspoons unsweetened cocoa powder

- 1 teaspoon espresso powder

Preparation

1- Place the nuts, butter and erythritol into a food processor. Pulse until the ingredients stick together and a paste forms.

2- Squeeze the dough into a 4-inch hinged pan and place it in the air fryer basket.

3- Set the temperature to 400 ° F and set the timer to 5 minutes.

4- When the timer rings remove the crust and let cool.

5- In a medium bowl, combine the cream cheese with the egg, vanilla extract, erythritol powder, cocoa powder and espresso powder until smooth.

6- Place the mixture on the nut crust in the oven and place in the basket of the air fryer.

7- Set the temperature to 300 ° F and set the timer to 10 minutes.

8- Once cooked, let cool 2 hours before serving.

Nutrition facts per serving

Calories: 535; Fat: 48.4 g; Protein: 11.6 g; Carb: 5.9 g; Fiber: 7.2 g

Mini Chocolate Chip Pan Cookie

Hands-On Time: **10 minutes**; *Cook Time:* **7 minutes**; *Yield:* **4 servings**.

Ingredients

- ½ cup blanched finely ground almond flour
- ¼ cup powdered erythritol
- 2 tablespoons unsalted butter, softened
- 1 large egg
- ½ teaspoon unflavored gelatin
- ½ teaspoon baking powder
- ½ teaspoon vanilla extract
- 2 tablespoons low-carb, sugar-free chocolate chips

Preparation

1- In a large bowl, mix almond flour and erythritol. Stir in butter, egg and gelatin until smooth.

2- Stir in the baking powder and vanilla, then stir in the chocolate chips. Pour the dough into a 6-inch round pan. Place the pan in the basket of the fryer.

3- Set the temperature to 300 ° F and set the timer to 7 minutes.

4- Once cooked, the top will be golden and a toothpick inserted in the center will come out clean. Cool for at least 10 minutes.

Nutrition facts per serving

Calories: 188

Fat: 15.7 g

Protein: 5.6 g

Carb: 2.3 g

Fiber: 2 g

Layered Peanut Butter Cheesecake Brownies

Hands-On Time: **20 minutes**; *Cook Time:* **35 minutes**; *Yield*: **6 servings**.

Ingredients

- ½ cup blanched finely ground almond flour

- 1 cup powdered erythritol, divided

- 2 tablespoons unsweetened cocoa powder

- ½ teaspoon baking powder

- ¼ cup unsalted butter, softened

- 2 large eggs divided

- 8 ounces full-fat cream cheese, softened

- ¼ cup heavy whipping cream

- 1 teaspoon vanilla extract

- 2 tablespoons no-sugar-added peanut butter

Preparation

1- In a large bowl, mix almond flour, ½-cup erythritol, cocoa powder and baking powder. Stir in the butter and an egg.

2- Place the mixture in a 6-inch round baking dish. Place the pan in the basket of the fryer.

3- Set the temperature to 300 ° F and set the timer to 20 minutes.

4- Once cooked, a toothpick inserted in the center will come out clean. Allow 20 minutes to cool and firm completely.

5- In large bowl, beat cream cheese, ½-cup erythritol, heavy cream, vanilla, peanut butter and remaining egg until frothy.

6- Pour the mixture over the cooled brownies. Place the pan in the basket of the fryer.

7- Set the temperature to 300 ° F and set the timer to 15 minutes.

8- Cheesecake will be slightly browned and usually firm, with a slight shake at the end. Let cool, then refrigerate 2 hours before serving.

Nutrition facts per serving

Calories: 347; Fat: 30.9 g; Protein: 8.3 g; Carb: 3.8 g; Fiber: 2 g

Coconut Flour Mug Cake

Hands-On Time: **5 minutes**; *Cook Time:* **25 minutes**; *Yield*: **1 serving**.

Ingredients

- 1 large egg

- 2 tablespoons coconut flour

- 2 tablespoons heavy whipping cream

- 2 tablespoons granular erythritol

- ¼ teaspoon vanilla extract

- ¼ teaspoon baking powder

Preparation

1- In a 4-inch ramekin, beat the egg and add the remaining ingredients. Stir until smooth. Place in the basket of the air fryer.

2- Set the temperature to 300 ° F and set the timer to 25 minutes. Once finished, a toothpick should come out clean. Enjoy as soon as you leave the ramekin with a spoon. Serve hot.

Nutrition facts per serving

Calories: 237

Fat: 16.4 g

Protein: 9.9 g

Carb: 5.7 g

Fiber: 5 g

Pumpkin Cookie with Cream Cheese Frosting

Hands-On Time: **10 minutes**; *Cook Time:* **7 minutes**; *Yield*: **6 servings**.

Ingredients

• ½ cup blanched finely ground almond flour

• ½ cup powdered erythritol, divided

• 2 tablespoons butter, softened

• 1 large egg

• ½ teaspoon unflavored gelatin

• ½ teaspoon baking powder

• ½ teaspoon vanilla extract

• ½ teaspoon pumpkin pie spice

• 2 tablespoons pure pumpkin purée

• ½ teaspoon ground cinnamon divided

• ¼ cup low-carb, sugar-free chocolate chips

• 3 ounces full-fat cream cheese, softened

Preparation

1- In a large bowl, mix the almond flour and ¼-cup erythritol. Stir in butter, egg and gelatin until smooth.

2- Stir in baking powder, vanilla, pumpkin pie spice, pumpkin puree and ¼-teaspoon cinnamon, then stir in chocolate chips.

3- Pour the dough into a 6-inch round pan and place the pan in the basket of the air fryer.

4- Set the temperature to 300 ° F and set the timer to 7 minutes.

5- Once cooked, the top will be golden and a toothpick inserted in the center will come out clean. Cool for at least 20 minutes.

6- To make the glaze: mix the cream cheese, ¼-teaspoon of remaining cinnamon and ¼-cup of erythritol in a large bowl. Using an electric mixer, beat until the mixture becomes foamy. Spread on the cooled biscuit. Decorate with extra cinnamon if desired.

Nutrition facts per serving

Calories: 199; Fat: 16.2 g; Protein: 4.8 g; Carb: 2.9 g; Fiber: 1.9 g

Caramel Monkey Bread

Hands-On Time: **15 minutes**; *Cook Time:* **12 minutes**; *Yield*: **6 servings**.

Ingredients

- ½ cup blanched finely ground almond flour

- ½ cup low-carb vanilla protein powder

- ¾ cup granular erythritol divided

- ½ teaspoon baking powder

- 8 tablespoons salted butter, melted and divided

- 1 ounce full-fat cream cheese, softened

- 1 large egg

- ¼ cup heavy whipping cream

- ½ teaspoon vanilla extract

Preparation

1- In a large bowl, mix almond flour, protein powder, ½-cup erythritol, baking powder, 5 tablespoons butter, cream cheese and eggs. A soft and sticky paste will form.

2- Place the dough in the freezer for 20 minutes. It will be firm enough to roll in balls. Wet your hands with warm water and roll in twelve balls. Place the balls in a round 6-inch baking dish.

3- In a medium skillet over medium heat, melt remaining butter with remaining erythritol. Lower the heat and continue to stir until the mixture becomes golden, then add the cream and vanilla. Remove from heat and let thicken for a few minutes while stirring.

4- While the mixture cools, place a baking dish in the basket of the air fryer.

5- Set the temperature to 320 ° F and set the timer to 6 minutes.

6- When the timer sounds return the monkey bread to a plate and return to the baking dish. Cook another 4 minutes until all peaks are brown.

7- Pour the caramel sauce over the monkey bread and cook another 2 minutes. Let cool completely before serving.

Nutrition facts per serving

Calories: 322; Fat: 24.5 g; Protein: 20.4 g; Carb: 2 g; Fiber: 1.7 g

Pan Peanut Butter Cookies

Hands-On Time: **5 minutes**; *Cook Time:* **8 minutes**; *Yield*: **8 servings**.

Ingredients

- 1 cup no-sugar-added smooth peanut butter

- ⅓ cup granular erythritol

- 1 large egg

- 1 teaspoon vanilla extract

Preparation

1- In a large bowl, combine all ingredients until smooth. Continue stirring for another 2 minutes and the mixture will begin to thicken.

2- Roll the mixture into eight balls and gently press to flatten them into 2-inch round discs.

3- Cut a piece of parchment suitable for your air fryer and place it in the basket. Place the cookies on the parchment, working in batches if necessary.

4- Set the temperature to 320 ° F and set the timer to 8 minutes.

5- Return the cookies after 6 minutes. Serve completely cooled.

Nutrition facts per serving

Calories: 210

Fat: 17.5 g

Protein: 8.8 g

Carb: 2.1 g

Fiber: 2 g

Cinnamon Cream Puffs

Hands-On Time: **15 minutes**; *Cook Time:* **6 minutes**; *Yield*: **8 puffs**.

Ingredients

• ½ cup blanched finely ground almond flour

• ½ cup low-carb vanilla protein powder

• ½ cup granular erythritol

• ½ teaspoon baking powder

• 1 large egg

• 5 tablespoons unsalted butter, melted

• 2 ounces full-fat cream cheese

• ¼ cup powdered erythritol

• ¼ teaspoon ground cinnamon

• 2 tablespoons heavy whipping cream

• ½ teaspoon vanilla extract

Preparation

1- In a large bowl, mix almond flour, protein powder, erythritol powder, baking powder, eggs and butter until soft dough forms.

2- Place the dough in the freezer for 20 minutes. Wet your hands with water and roll the dough into eight balls.

3- Cut out a piece of parchment suitable for your air fryer basket. When working in batches if necessary, place the balls of dough in the basket of the air fryer above the parchment.

4- Set the temperature to 380 ° F and set the timer to 6 minutes.

5- Return the cabbages to half the time.

6- When the timer sounds remove the puffs and allow them to cool.

7- In medium bowl, beat cream cheese, erythritol powder, cinnamon, cream and vanilla until smooth.

8- Place the mixture in a pastry bag or storage bag with the cut end. Cut a small hole in the bottom of each puff and fill it with a little cream mixture.

9- Store in an airtight container for up to 2 days in the refrigerator.

Nutrition facts per serving: *Calories: 178; Fat: 12.1 g; Protein: 14.9 g; Carb: 1.3 g; Fiber: 1.3 g*

Conclusion

One of the keys to any successful diet or lifestyle change has always been recipes based on the principles of healthy eating. I'm sure there are many ways to achieve ketosis and achieve your weight loss goal. However, you certainly do not want to get there by simply having the same old dishes over and over again.

Variety is the title of the game here, which is crucial to ensuring the sustainability of the ketogenic diet. With the tasty and delicious recipes found in this keto cookbook, they will be useful additions for anyone on a keto diet at any stage of their journey. I have not seen anyone complaining about having too many easy, but delicious recipes!

We are all fans of good food. It's not just our fuel, it's our mood manipulator. We all know how important it is to eat healthily when we are so hungry that we forget about health. We often eat what we find most accessible. So, why not make the good things easier to have? I know things do not always go as planned; You will always find other attractions. But from now on, I think you can trust this book to defeat other because you know that you can make the same thing healthier with the least amount of time possible. I certainly do not boast about it. Many chefs have confirmed that an air fryer can make it healthier and faster. It's not even an oven alternative; it is unique by its own cooking. There are many recipes we have now and I guess it will help us experiment a little deeper with our tastes. It's also something to trust on vacation. As he always cooks food thoroughly; so you can count on that when you relax in a recreational vehicle with your favorite music. For all these reasons and many more, I am particularly fond of the air fryer and the taste that the recipes will serve.

We have arrived at this stage and I am delighted that you have chosen to take the necessary steps for your ketogenic journey. I hope this book and its contents will be able to give you concrete value for your progress towards nutritional ketosis.

More importantly, I hope the book has also given you a newfound confidence and strengthened your commitment to staying on a healthy diet.

I will be very happy to know your honest opinions. Criticism is always the motivation for the next job. Please tell me what you think.

Live healthy, live hard.

About the Author

Michèle COHEN is a nutritionist, certified coach in humanistic approaches, and author. Michèle discovered a passion for nutrition when she improvised healthy modifications to muffin recipes. She is a woman of depth, passionate about research, knowledge, and balance. In fact, she has a long track record of more than 18 years in the field of nutrition and coaching in life.

Michèle is a graduate of the University of Montreal and practices in a liberal cabinet in Laval, as well as in France in Cannes.

Over the years, Michèle has refined her approach of helping people to rediscover the meaning that unites them to live.

In addition to using her creativity in healthy nutrition and a humanistic approach, Michèle is a lover of fitness and swimming. She is the first to say that keeping fit and eating well should be done for pleasure and not for chores!

To live his ideal…

The miracle of advancement is first and foremost, this desire, this vision that drives us and pushes us to go forward.

The purpose sets us on the road; it's the engine that starts … like when driving on an unknown road with a destination in mind.

26919579R00117

Made in the USA
San Bernardino, CA
23 February 2019